FATTY LIVER DIET COOKBOOK

Revitalize Your Liver and Enjoy 2000 Days of Easy, Proven Recipes for Increased Energy and Weight Loss

Along With an 8-Week Meal Plan for a Healthier Liver

MARYEM PETTERSON

FATTY LIVER DIET COOKBOOK

Table of Contents

CHAPTER 8. SALADS AND SIDES RECIPES 51

CHAPTER 9. DINNER RECIPES 58

CHAPTER 10. SNACKS RECIPES 69

CHAPTER 11. SPECIAL VEGETABLE RECIPES 75

CHAPTER 12. DESSERT RECIPES 83

8 - WEEK MEAL PLAN 87

CONVERSION CHART 95

RECIPES INDEX 97

CONCLUSION 100

Introduction

The liver, an essential organ located on the upper-right side of the belly, is critical to the body's overall health and well-being. Without a doubt, it is the largest internal organ in the human body. The liver's functions are diverse and essential to the body's proper functioning, with two primary roles standing out: detoxification and nutrient processing.

One of the liver's primary functions is to eliminate poisons and toxic compounds from the bloodstream. After absorbing nutrients from the food we consume, the blood from the digestive system passes through the liver for filtration. This process ensures that any potentially harmful substances are neutralized and eliminated, safeguarding the body from the damaging effects of toxins.

However, in certain cases, the liver's health can be compromised due to various factors, leading to a condition known as fatty liver disease or steatosis. This disease is common in Western countries, affecting roughly one out of every 10 people. While it is natural for the liver to contain some fat, if the fat content exceeds 10% of the liver's weight, it is classified as fatty liver, and further complications may arise.

Fatty liver disease can be relatively harmless, with no substantial liver damage.

However, in some instances, the accumulation of excess fat can lead to inflammation in the liver, resulting in a condition called steatohepatitis. This inflammatory state can cause significant harm to the liver and should not be taken lightly. In cases where the inflammation is associated with alcohol abuse, it is termed alcoholic steatohepatitis. Otherwise, when the condition is unrelated to alcohol consumption, it is referred to as non-alcoholic steatohepatitis, or NASH.

Chronic inflammation in the liver can lead to a concerning and potentially life-threatening condition known as cirrhosis.

Over time, the liver may become scarred and hardened due to prolonged inflammation, hindering its proper functioning. Cirrhosis is a severe condition and often culminates in liver failure, which necessitates immediate medical attention and potentially a liver transplant. It is important to note that NASH ranks among the top three leading causes of cirrhosis, emphasizing the seriousness of this liver disease.

Given the seriousness of liver illnesses, such as fatty liver disease and its potential development to NASH and cirrhosis, it is critical to adopt a healthy lifestyle that includes a balanced diet, frequent exercise, and avoiding excessive alcohol intake. Early detection and proactive management of liver-related disorders can considerably improve prognosis, ensuring a healthier and better quality of life.

Consulting a healthcare professional for regular check-ups and taking preventive measures can go a long way in preserving the health of this vital organ and the overall well-being of an individual.

Chapter 1. Understanding Fatty Liver

Fatty liver, also known as hepatic steatosis, is caused by an abnormal accumulation of fat within the liver cells. While a modest amount of fat in the liver is normal and necessary for its functioning, an excessive buildup of fat can be dangerous.

As the 2nd largest organ in the body, the liver plays crucial roles in processing nutrients obtained from the food we consume and filtering harmful substances from the bloodstream. It metabolizes fats, converting them into energy or storing them for later use. Additionally, the liver aids in breaking down carbohydrates and proteins and serves as a central detoxification hub, removing toxins and harmful compounds from the blood.

When fat builds up in the liver in excess, it can cause inflammation, a condition known as steatohepatitis. Over time, this inflammation can harm liver cells and cause scar tissue, a condition known as fibrosis. If left untreated and the liver remains exposed to factors contributing to fatty liver, such as obesity or metabolic disorders, the fibrosis can advance to a more severe stage called cirrhosis. In cirrhosis, extensive scarring disrupts the liver's normal functioning, potentially leading to liver failure.

Fatty liver disease is categorized into 2 main types: alcoholic fatty liver disease (AFLD) and nonalcoholic fatty liver disease (NAFLD). AFLD occurs in individuals who consume extreme amounts of alcohol regularly, as alcohol is toxic to liver cells and can trigger fat accumulation and inflammation in the liver.

NAFLD, on the other hand, develops in persons who drink little to no alcohol. It is closely associated with conditions such as obesity, type 2 diabetes, insulin resistance, & metabolic syndrome. NAFLD is presently the most prevalent liver disease in Western countries, affecting a significant proportion of the population. Studies from 2017 estimate that NAFLD impacts approximately 25% - 30% of individuals in the United States and Europe.

NAFLD can progress to a more severe form known as nonalcoholic steatohepatitis (NASH). NASH is characterized by liver inflammation and damage to liver cells, which can lead to fibrosis and cirrhosis over time. The development of NASH is particularly concerning, as it increases the risk of complications such as liver cancer and liver failure. Early detection and appropriate management are essential in addressing fatty liver conditions and preventing their advancement to more severe stages. Regular medical check-ups & consultations with healthcare professionals are crucial for monitoring the condition and devising personalized treatment plans.

Causes and Triggering Factors of Fatty Liver

Excessive calorie consumption can have adverse effects on our bodies, and one of the consequences is the accumulation of fat in the liver. Normally, the liver plays a crucial role in processing and breaking down fats, but when it is overwhelmed by an excessive intake of calories, it struggles to cope, leading to the storage of excess fat within the liver tissue. This condition is known as fatty liver or hepatic steatosis.

Several underlying factors contribute to the development of fatty liver, making it a multifaceted condition. One of the significant risk factors is obesity, where an excessive amount of body fat puts extra strain on the liver and hinders its proper functioning. Similarly, diabetes, a metabolic disorder characterized by high blood sugar levels, can also contribute to fatty liver due to the way it affects fat metabolism in the body.

High triglyceride levels, which are a type of fat in the blood, can be another contributing factor to fatty liver development. Elevated triglycerides often result from an unhealthy diet, sedentary lifestyle, or genetic predisposition, and they can exacerbate the accumulation of fat in the liver.

Apart from lifestyle-related factors, certain behaviors can also lead to fatty liver. Alcohol misuse is a well-known cause of liver damage, and long-term alcohol intake can result in alcoholic fatty liver disease. Additionally, rapid weight loss, especially through crash diets or extreme methods, and malnutrition can also trigger fatty liver, as the liver may not have enough time or resources to process the sudden changes in fat metabolism.

Surprisingly, some individuals develop fatty liver even in the absence of the usual risk factors, such as obesity, diabetes, high triglycerides, alcohol abuse, or rapid weight loss. This form of fatty liver, often referred to as non-alcoholic fatty liver disease (NAFLD), is a complex condition that may be influenced by genetic factors, insulin resistance, and inflammation in the body.

Fatty liver is a condition that arises from the accumulation of fat in the liver due to various factors, such as excessive calorie consumption, obesity, diabetes, high triglycerides, alcohol abuse, rapid weight loss, malnutrition, and other underlying genetic or metabolic issues. Managing and preventing fatty liver involve adopting a healthy lifestyle, balanced diet, regular exercise, and addressing any underlying medical conditions to support liver health and overall well-being If you feel you have fatty liver or other symptoms, you should see a doctor for an accurate diagnosis and treatment.

Prevalence and Risk Factors

Fatty liver can affect people of various ages and body types, it is true that a significant proportion of fatty liver patients tend to be middle-aged and overweight. However, it is essential to note that not all cases fit this profile, as the disease can also impact individuals who do not fall into these categories.

Several risk factors have been closely associated with the development of fatty liver disease. These factors all play a part in increasing the chances of someone developing this illness. The following are the most frequently linked risk factors:

• Overweight: Being overweight is a significant risk factor for fatty liver disease. Specifically, individuals with a body mass index (BMI) ranging from 25 to 30 are at an increased risk of developing the condition.

• Obesity: Obesity, defined by a BMI above 30, presents an even higher risk of fatty liver disease. The more excess body weight a person carries, the more strain is placed on the liver, making it more susceptible to fat accumulation.

• Diabetes: People with diabetes, especially type 2 diabetes, are more prone to fatty liver disease. The mechanism involves insulin resistance, which interferes with the liver's ability to regulate fat storage and metabolism, leading to fat accumulation.

• Elevated Triglyceride Levels: High levels of triglycerides in the blood can contribute to fatty liver disease. Triglycerides are a type of fat that the liver produces, and when they are excessively elevated, the liver's ability to handle fat processing can be overwhelmed.

It's important to highlight that while these are the most common risk factors, other factors can also play a role in the development of fatty liver disease. Genetics, certain medications, rapid weight loss, excessive alcohol consumption, and certain medical conditions can all contribute to the condition.

Differentiation of Alcoholic and Non-Alcoholic Liver Steatosis

Non-alcoholic fatty liver disease (NAFLD) is a prevalent and significant health concern worldwide, responsible for a majority of chronic liver disease cases. It affects about 25-30% of the global population. NAFLD was first identified as a distinct condition from alcohol-related fatty liver disease (ALD) in 1980. Despite their conceptual separation, both NAFLD and ALD share commonalities in their underlying mechanisms, genetic and epigenetic factors, and are often found to coexist in some individuals. The spectrum of histological features for both diseases ranges from simple steatosis (fatty liver) to more severe conditions like steatohepatitis (inflammation) and cirrhosis (scarring of the liver).

Distinguishing NAFLD from ALD has historically been based on the amount of alcohol consumed, and an arbitrary threshold was set to make the differentiation. However, some experts have proposed a new approach to diagnose NAFLD, which does not solely rely on excluding alcohol consumption as a prerequisite criterion. This recognizes the possibility that some individuals may have a dual etiology for fatty liver, involving both alcohol and non-alcohol-related factors.

The relationship between moderate alcohol consumption & the severity of NAFLD remains uncertain. Although certain studies have hinted at potential protective effects of moderate alcohol intake, the current evidence indicates that there is no established safe threshold for alcohol consumption in the context of NAFLD. The interaction between alcohol consumption, obesity, and metabolic dysfunction seems to have a synergistic impact, significantly elevating the risk of liver disease progression in individuals with NAFLD and metabolic syndrome. Additionally, this combination also influences the occurrence of hepatocellular carcinoma, a form of liver cancer. As a result, it is crucial for individuals with NAFLD to exercise caution regarding alcohol consumption, and medical advice should be sought to understand the potential risks and implications on their liver health.

Reduction of Alcohol Consumption

In both NAFLD and ALD, it is crucial to consider alcohol avoidance as an essential aspect of treatment and management. For individuals with NAFLD, avoiding alcohol is recommended because alcohol can worsen liver inflammation and contribute to disease progression, especially in those with underlying metabolic risk factors. Even moderate alcohol consumption may have harmful effects on the liver in the context of NAFLD.

For those with ALD, alcohol avoidance is even more critical. The primary treatment for ALD is complete abstinence from alcohol. By abstaining from alcohol, the liver has a chance to repair itself and reduce the fat accumulation, inflammation, and scarring caused by excessive alcohol consumption. Continued alcohol consumption in ALD patients can result in severe liver damage and life-threatening consequences.

For individuals with ALD who have been heavy and prolonged alcohol consumers, abrupt alcohol cessation can lead to alcohol withdrawal syndrome. Alcohol withdrawal syndrome refers to a spectrum of symptoms that can arise when an individual who is dependent on alcohol abruptly ceases drinking. These symptoms can range from mild to severe & may encompass anxiety, tremors, perspiration, nausea, vomiting, seizures, and in extreme cases, delirium tremens, a critical and potentially life-threatening form of withdrawal. In severe cases, alcohol withdrawal requires medical attention and management, and inpatient treatment may be necessary.

If you or someone you know is experiencing alcohol dependence or is concerned about fatty liver disease, it is essential to seek medical advice and support. A healthcare practitioner can advise you on how to manage your alcohol use and treat you for fatty liver disease. Remember that early intervention and lifestyle modifications are critical to limiting the advancement of liver disease and promoting overall liver health.

Chapter 2. Managing Fatty Liver Through Diet

Lifestyle Changes for Fatty Liver

Implementing lifestyle changes is crucial for individuals with fatty liver disease to reduce and manage their symptoms effectively. Fatty liver disease, commonly known as hepatic steatosis, is a common liver ailment marked by excessive fat accumulation in liver cells. While it can be a benign condition, it can also progress to more severe stages, such as nonalcoholic steatohepatitis (NASH) or alcoholic liver disease (ALD), which can lead to serious liver damage if not managed properly. Lifestyle modifications, particularly in the areas of diet and exercise, play a fundamental role in preventing and managing fatty liver disease.

Adjusting Calorie Intake: For individuals with non-alcoholic fatty liver disease (NAFLD), weight loss is a key strategy to reduce fat accumulation in the liver. Studies have shown that even a modest weight loss of about 5% to 10% can lead to a significant improvement in liver health. The recommended calorie intake for a person with NAFLD varies depending on age, gender, activity level, and underlying health issues. In general, it is recommended to either consume about 1,200–1,500 calories per day or reduce their daily intake by 500–1000 calories to achieve weight loss. However, individualized dietary plans are crucial to ensure that the nutritional needs of the person are met while promoting weight loss.

For people with alcohol-related fatty liver disease (ALD), proper nutrition is essential due to the risk of malnutrition associated with the condition. Alcohol can interfere with nutrient absorption and lead to deficiencies in vitamins and minerals. Research suggests that an optimal caloric intake for individuals with ALD is around 2,000 calories per day, incorporating about 1.2 to 1.5 grams of protein per kilogram of body weight. Adequate protein intake is required for liver cell regeneration and liver function. Additionally, it is beneficial for individuals with fatty liver disease to eat smaller, more frequent meals with shorter intervals between them. This eating pattern can aid in improving food absorption, maintaining stable blood sugar levels, and reducing the burden on the liver during digestion.

Being Physically Active: Regular physical exercise offers numerous benefits for everyone, and it is especially beneficial for people with fatty liver disease in managing their symptoms. Exercise not only plays a vital role in facilitating weight loss but also has a positive impact on liver health by enhancing insulin sensitivity and reducing liver inflammation. For individuals with NAFLD, the American Gastroenterological Association (AGA) recommends engaging in at least 150 to 300 mins of moderate aerobic exercise or 75 to 150 mins of vigorous exercise per week.

Incorporating physical activity into daily routines can be achieved through simple lifestyle adjustments, making it more feasible for individuals to stay active. For instance, replacing prolonged sitting with using a standing workstation can promote continuous movement throughout the day. Incorporating stretches and light exercises in the morning or during leisure time, such as while watching TV, can also contribute significantly to overall activity levels.

Choosing to take the stairs instead of the elevator, walking or cycling for short distances, and participating in gardening or other recreational activities are additional ways to integrate physical activity into everyday life without necessitating a dedicated time slot for a full workout. These small but consistent efforts can add up to substantial health benefits, supporting weight management and contributing to better liver health in individuals with fatty liver disease.

Limiting Added Sugars and Processed Foods: High sugar and processed food consumption is strongly associated with fatty liver disease, especially NAFLD. Added sugars & refined carbohydrates can lead to spikes in blood sugar levels & contribute to insulin resistance, which is a risk factor for NAFLD. Reducing the intake of sugary beverages, sweets, and processed foods is crucial for managing the condition. Individuals with fatty liver should instead focus on eating full, unprocessed foods and, in moderation, use natural sources of sweetness such as fruits or natural sweeteners such as honey or maple syrup.

Incorporating Liver-Friendly Foods: Certain foods are known to be beneficial for liver health and can be incorporated into the diet to support liver function. Some liver-friendly foods include:

• Individuals with fatty liver should instead focus on eating full, unprocessed foods and, in moderation, use natural sources of sweetness such as fruits or natural sweeteners such as honey or maple syrup.

• Individuals with fatty liver should instead focus on eating full, unprocessed foods and, in moderation, use natural sources of sweetness such as fruits or natural sweeteners such as honey or maple syrup. These fatty acids can be beneficial in reducing fat accumulation within the liver and promoting better liver health.

• Studies have suggested a potential link between moderate coffee consumption & a reduced risk of liver diseases like NAFLD and ALD. Including coffee in a liver-friendly diet may have protective effects on the liver.

• Green tea is rich in antioxidants that can play a role in shielding the liver from oxidative stress and inflammation, contributing to improved liver function.

• Nuts & seeds are excellent sources of healthy fats & antioxidants, both of which are valuable in supporting overall liver health and protecting against oxidative damage.

• Garlic has been the subject of research indicating its anti-inflammatory and antioxidant effects, which could be advantageous for individuals with fatty liver disease, aiding in mitigating inflammation and oxidative stress in the liver.

Limiting Alcohol Consumption: For individuals with alcohol-related fatty liver disease (ALD), the most critical lifestyle change is to limit or completely eliminate alcohol consumption. Alcohol is toxic to liver cells & can exacerbate liver damage. If alcohol is a contributing factor to fatty liver disease, seeking support and treatment for alcohol dependency is essential for successful management.

Importance of Diet and Nutrition

The importance of diet and nutrition cannot be overstated when it comes to managing and preventing fatty liver disease, encompassing both Alcoholic Fatty Liver Disease (AFD) and Non-Alcoholic Fatty Liver Disease (NAFLD). By making appropriate dietary choices, individuals can enhance liver health, decrease fat buildup in the liver, and safeguard against the advancement of more severe conditions like non-alcoholic steatohepatitis (NASH) and cirrhosis. Here are key reasons elucidating the significance of diet and nutrition for fatty liver:

1. Weight Management: Weight plays a crucial role in NAFLD risk, making weight loss a fundamental aspect of managing fatty liver. A balanced and controlled-calorie diet aids in achieving and maintaining a healthy weight, thereby reducing the strain on the liver and improving its function.

2. Insulin Sensitivity: Insulin resistance is commonly linked to NAFLD, and certain diets, rich in refined carbohydrates and sugars, can worsen insulin resistance. A carbohydrate-balanced diet that emphasizes complex carbs from fruits, vegetables, and whole grains can increase insulin sensitivity. Reduced Fat Accumulation: Dietary choices directly impact fat accumulation in the liver. Diets high in saturated fats & trans fats are associated with increased liver fat deposition, whereas diets rich in healthy fats, like monounsaturated fats and omega-3 fatty acids, may help reduce fat accumulation.

3. Antioxidants and Anti-inflammatory Effects: A diet abundant in antioxidants from fruits, vegetables, and plant-based foods can alleviate oxidative stress and inflammation in the liver. This protection is vital for preserving liver cells and supporting overall liver function.

4. Nutrient Support: Specific nutrients, such as vitamin E, have demonstrated potential benefits in managing fatty liver disease. Including nutrient-dense foods in the diet ensures that the body receives essential vitamins and minerals essential for optimal liver health.

5. Impact on Lipid Profile: Diet influences blood lipid levels, including cholesterol and triglycerides, which are associated with NAFLD. Making dietary modifications can improve lipid profiles and reduce the risk of fatty liver progression.

6. Gut Health: The gut microbiota plays a role in liver health, and certain dietary components like prebiotics and probiotics can positively influence gut health, potentially impacting fatty liver disease.

7. Overall Health & Well-being: A healthy diet not only benefits the liver but also supports overall health and well-being. It boosts energy levels, enhances the immune system, and reduces the risk of other chronic diseases such as type 2 diabetes & cardiovascular disease, which are often associated with fatty liver.

Diet and nutrition are pivotal in managing fatty liver disease. A well-balanced diet that promotes weight loss (if necessary), improves insulin sensitivity, reduces fat accumulation, and provides essential nutrients and antioxidants can significantly impact liver health and potentially reverse or halt the progression of fatty liver disease. For individuals with fatty liver, it is essential to collaborate with healthcare professionals or registered dietitians to develop personalized nutrition plans tailored to their specific needs and health conditions.

Weight Control and Fatty Liver

NAFLD is a condition in which excess fat accumulates in the liver of individuals who consume little to no alcohol. It is the most common liver disease in the western world, affecting a substantial number of adults in the United States. NAFLD typically progresses slowly and often goes unnoticed as it doesn't cause noticeable symptoms, and liver test results may appear normal. It is frequently detected incidentally during imaging exams performed for other reasons, such as CT scans or MRIs.

The disease can evolve into a more serious form known as nonalcoholic steatohepatitis (NASH) in some cases. NASH involves inflammation and scarring of the liver and poses a greater risk of complications. Unlike NAFLD, NASH may cause abnormal liver test results in some patients, indicating liver damage. It is essential to diagnose NASH early as it puts individuals at a higher risk of liver cancer and faster development of cirrhosis, a condition characterized by extensive scarring that impairs liver function and can lead to liver failure.

The primary treatment approach for most people with NAFLD and NASH involves weight loss. Shedding excess weight is effective in reducing liver fat, inflammation, and scarring. A weight loss of at least 3-5 percent of body weight is necessary to begin seeing improvements in liver fat, while a greater weight loss of around 10 percent is needed to address inflammation and scarring.

Weight loss is best achieved through a combination of a low-calorie diet and increased physical activity. Healthcare providers, including doctors, dietitians, and endocrinologists, can collaborate with individuals to create personalized weight-loss programs that suit their needs and health conditions. In cases where obesity or obesity-related medical problems are severe, bariatric surgery may be recommended as an option to facilitate significant weight loss and improve NAFLD or NASH.

For those who may not qualify for or prefer not to undergo bariatric surgery, new endoscopic techniques to assist with weight loss may be considered. One such technique involves placing a balloon in the stomach to reduce food intake and limit calorie consumption. While not established as a standard treatment for NAFLD or NASH, this method can serve as a temporary measure to kickstart weight loss. However, maintaining a healthy lifestyle after balloon removal is essential to avoid weight regain.

Regular monitoring of the condition by a physician specializing in liver disease is crucial for individuals with NAFLD or NASH. Monitoring helps assess disease progression, identify potential complications, and evaluate the effectiveness of the chosen treatment approach.

Shopping List

What to Eat

Opting for appropriate dietary choices can aid in diminishing fat accumulation in the liver, easing inflammation, and promoting overall liver well-being. Below are some foods that prove advantageous for a fatty liver diet:

1. **Fresh Fruits & Vegetables:** Rich in antioxidants, vitamins, and minerals, fruits and vegetables bolster liver health and reduce oxidative stress. Incorporate a variety of colorful fruits and leafy greens into your diet to obtain essential nutrients.

2. **Whole Grains:** Including brown rice, quinoa, oats, & whole wheat in your meals provides fiber and complex carbohydrates, which help regulate blood sugar levels & enhance insulin sensitivity.

3. **Lean Proteins:** Choose lean protein sources such as skinless poultry, fish, tofu, and lentils. These proteins are low in saturated fats and contribute to maintaining muscle mass while undergoing weight loss.

4. **Healthy Fats:** Integrate healthy fats from avocados, nuts, seeds, and olive oil into your diet.

These fats contain monounsaturated and polyunsaturated fatty acids, which are beneficial to the heart and liver.

5. **Fatty Fish:** Fatty fish, such as salmon, mackerel, and sardines, are high in omega-3 fatty acids, which have anti-inflammatory qualities and may help reduce liver fat.

6. **Low-Fat Dairy:** Opt for low-fat or non-fat dairy products to reduce saturated fat intake while still obtaining essential nutrients like calcium and vitamin D.

7. **Herbal Teas:** Green tea and dandelion root tea, among others, boast antioxidant properties that promote liver health and aid in digestion.

8. **Flaxseeds:** Flaxseeds are rich in fiber & omega-3 fatty acids. To add nutritional value to your yogurt, oatmeal, or smoothies, sprinkle ground flaxseeds on top.

9. **Garlic:** Garlic has demonstrated anti-inflammatory and antioxidant effects that can be beneficial for individuals with fatty liver disease.

10. **Cruciferous Vegetables:** Broccoli, cauliflower, and Brussels sprouts have chemicals that help the liver detoxify.

11. **Beets:** Beets contain betaine, a compound that may aid in reducing liver fat and inflammation.

12. **Sweet Potatoes:** Rich in fiber and antioxidants like beta-carotene, sweet potatoes are beneficial for liver health.

13. **Cinnamon:** Cinnamon is believed to improve insulin sensitivity and regulate blood sugar levels.

14. **Turmeric:** Curcumin, the main ingredient in turmeric, has anti-inflammatory qualities that may benefit liver function.

15. **Water:** Ensuring proper hydration is crucial for liver health. Strive to stay well-hydrated by consuming an ample amount of water throughout the day.

What to Avoid

It is critical to avoid certain foods in a fatty liver diet since they can contribute to liver fat formation and damage liver function. The following foods should be avoided:

16. **Sugary Foods and Beverages:** Avoid sugary sodas, fruit juices with added sugars, candies, cakes, cookies, and other high-sugar foods. Excess sugar consumption can cause fat formation in the liver and aggravate insulin resistance.

17. **Refined Carbohydrates:** Limit your intake of refined grains such as white bread, white rice, and pasta, which can induce blood sugar increases and lead to fatty liver.

18. **High-Fat Foods:** Avoid saturated and trans fat-rich foods such as fatty cuts of meat, fried dishes, full-fat dairy products, and processed snacks. These fats can lead to liver inflammation and worsen liver function.

19. **Processed Meats:** Cut back on processed meats like bacon, sausages, and deli meats, which contain high levels of unhealthy fats and additives that can harm the liver.

20. **Alcohol:** For individuals with non-alcoholic fatty liver disease (NAFLD), it is crucial to avoid alcohol completely, as it can exacerbate liver damage.

21. **High-Fructose Corn Syrup (HFCS):** Many processed foods and sweetened beverages include HFCS. It is very dangerous to the liver and should be avoided.

22. **Added Sugars:** Be cautious of foods with added sugars in their ingredients list, including sauces, dressings, and packaged snacks.

23. **Excessive Salt:** Reduce salt intake, as excessive sodium can lead to fluid retention & increase the risk of liver damage.

24. **High-Cholesterol Foods:** Limit foods high in cholesterol, such as organ meats, shellfish, and high-fat dairy products, as they can contribute to fatty deposits in the liver.

25. **Trans Fats:** Avoid foods containing trans fats, often found in some margarines, baked goods, and fast foods. Trans fats are harmful to heart health and can worsen fatty liver disease.

26. **Carbonated and Sugary Beverages:** Avoid carbonated drinks and sugary beverages like energy drinks and sweetened teas, as they are high in empty calories and sugar.

27. **Excessive Caffeine:** While moderate consumption of caffeine is generally safe, excessive intake may stress the liver. It's best to moderate coffee and energy drink consumption.

28. **Artificial Sweeteners:** There is some evidence indicating that artificial sweeteners may not be advantageous for liver health. As a result, it may be recommended to limit their usage until more research is completed.

29. **Excessive Red Meat:** A high consumption of red meat has been linked to an increased risk of fatty liver. It's best to consume it in moderation and opt for lean cuts.

30. **High-Sodium Foods:** Reducing the intake of foods high in sodium is crucial to prevent fluid retention and maintain optimal liver health. It is advised to limit the eating of processed and salty foods.

Chapter 3. Breakfast Recipes

Avocado Toast with Poached Egg

Preparation time: five mins

Cooking time: five mins

Servings: one

Ingredients:

• one piece whole-grain bread

• one ripe avocado, mashed

• one poached egg

• Salt and pepper as required

Directions:

1. Toast the whole-grain bread until it's crisp.
2. Spread the mashed avocado on your toasted bread.

3. Top with a poached egg and season using salt and pepper.

4. Serve instantly.

Per serving: Calories: 300 kcal; Fat: 15gm; Carbs: 20gm; Protein: 15gm

Oatmeal with Fresh Berries

Preparation time: five mins

Cooking time: five mins

Servings: one

Ingredients:

• half teacup rolled oats

• one teacup almond milk (unsweetened)

• half teacup fresh mixed berries (e.g., blueberries, strawberries, raspberries)

• one tbsp honey or maple syrup (optional)

• one tbsp chopped nuts (e.g., almonds, walnuts) for garnish

Directions:

1. Inside your small saucepot, raise the almond milk to a simmer at middling temp.

2. Stir in the rolled oats then cook for around three-five mins, till the oats are soft and the solution thickens.

3. Take out the oatmeal from heat and transfer to a container.

4. Top with fresh mixed berries and drizzle with honey or maple syrup if desired.

5. Garnish with chopped nuts.

6. Serve warm.

Per serving: Calories: 300 kcal; Fat: 10gm; Carbs: 45gm; Protein: 8gm

Greek Yogurt Parfait with Nuts and Honey

Preparation time: ten mins

Cooking time: zero mins

Servings: one

Ingredients:

• one teacup plain Greek yogurt (low-fat or fat-free)

• half teacup fresh fruit (e.g., mixed berries, sliced peaches)

• one tbsp chopped nuts (e.g., almonds, walnuts)

• one tsp honey

Directions:

1. In your glass or container, layer the Greek yogurt, fresh fruit, and chopped nuts.

2. Drizzle honey over the top.

3. Repeat the layers if desired.

4. Serve chilled.

Per serving: Calories: 250 kcal; Fat: 5gm; Carbs: 30gm; Protein: 20gm

Quinoa Breakfast Bowl with Almond Milk

Preparation time: ten mins

Cooking time: fifteen mins

Servings: two

Ingredients:

- half teacup quinoa, rinsed
- one teacup almond milk (unsweetened)
- half teacup fresh fruit (e.g., sliced bananas, berries)
- one tbsp chopped nuts (e.g., almonds, pecans)
- one tsp honey or maple syrup (optional)

Directions:

1. Inside your saucepot, raise the almond milk to a boil at middling temp.

2. Stir in the quinoa, lower the heat, cover, then simmer for around fifteen mins or 'til the quinoa is cooked then the liquid is immersed.

3. Take out the quinoa from temp. and allow it to relax for a few mins.

4. Split the quinoa into two containers and top with fresh fruit and chopped nuts.

5. Drizzle using honey or maple syrup if anticipated.

6. Serve warm.

Per serving: Calories: 300 kcal; Fat: 10gm; Carbs: 45gm; Protein: 10gm

Vegetable Frittata with Egg Whites

Preparation time: ten mins

Cooking time: fifteen mins

Servings: two

Ingredients:

- four egg whites
- half teacup chopped mixed vegetables (e.g., bell peppers, spinach, onions)
- one tbsp olive oil
- Salt and pepper as required

Directions:

1. Inside your container, whisk the egg whites till frothy. Season with salt and pepper.

2. Warm olive oil in your non-stick griddle at middling temp.

3. Include the chopped vegetables and sauté till they soften.

4. Pour the whisked egg whites over the vegetables in the griddle.

5. Cook for around five-seven mins or till the egg whites are set.

6. Cut the frittata into wedges and serve.

Per serving: Calories: 150 kcal; Fat: 6gm; Carbs: 6gm; Protein: 15gm

Chia Seed Pudding with Fruit Compote

Preparation time: five mins (plus overnight soaking)

Cooking time: ten mins

Servings: two

Ingredients:

- quarter teacup chia seeds
- one teacup almond milk (unsweetened)
- one teacup mixed fresh fruit (e.g., berries, mango, kiwi)
- one tbsp honey or maple syrup (optional)

Directions:

1. Inside your container, mix the chia seeds and almond milk. Stir well and allow it to relax for five mins.

2. Stir again to break up any clumps, cover, then refrigerate overnight.

3. In the morning, prepare the fruit compote by gently heating the mixed fresh fruit inside a small

saucepot at low temp. If anticipated, you may include honey or maple syrup for sweetness.

4. Stir the chia seed pudding and divide it into two serving containers.

5. Top with the warm fruit compote.

6. Serve chilled.

Per serving: Calories: 200 kcal; Fat: 8gm; Carbs: 30gm; Protein: 5gm

Whole Grain Pancakes with Fresh Fruit Toppings

Preparation time: ten mins

Cooking time: fifteen mins

Servings: two

Ingredients:

• one teacup whole grain pancake mix (check the label for no added saturated fats)

• three-quarter teacup almond milk (unsweetened)

• Fresh fruit toppings (e.g., sliced strawberries, blueberries)

• one tbsp pure maple syrup

Directions:

1. Prepare the pancake batter using the package instructions, substituting almond milk for regular milk.

2. Warm your non-stick griddle at middling temp. and mildly grease it using cooking spray or a small amount of olive oil.

3. Pour the pancake batter onto your griddle to form pancakes of your desired size.

4. Cook each side till bubbles form on the surface and the edges are mildly cooked. Turn then cook the all sides till golden brown.

5. Serve the pancakes topped with fresh fruit and a spray of pure maple syrup.

Per serving: Calories: 300 kcal; Fat: 5gm; Carbs: 50gm; Protein: 8gm

Veggie Omelet with Spinach and Tomatoes

Preparation time: ten mins

Cooking time: ten mins

Servings: one

Ingredients:

• three egg whites

• half teacup fresh spinach leaves

• half teacup diced tomatoes

• quarter teacup diced onions

• quarter teacup diced bell peppers

• Salt and pepper as required

• one tsp olive oil

Directions:

1. Inside your container, whisk the egg whites till frothy. Season with salt and pepper.

2. In your non-stick griddle, warm the olive oil at middling temp.

3. Include the diced onions and bell peppers. Sauté till softened.

4. Include the spinach and diced tomatoes, and cook till the spinach wilts.

5. Pour the whisked egg whites over the veggies in the griddle.

6. Cook till the egg whites are set and the omelet is mildly browned on the bottom.

7. Carefully wrap the omelet in half then slide it onto a plate to serve.

Per serving: Calories: 200 kcal; Fat: 8gm; Carbs: 10gm; Protein: 20gm

Brown Rice Porridge with Cinnamon and Apples

Preparation time: five mins

Cooking time: twenty mins

Servings: two

Ingredients:

- half teacup brown rice, rinsed
- one and half teacups water
- half teacup almond milk (unsweetened)
- half tsp ground cinnamon
- one apple, cubed
- one tbsp chopped nuts (e.g., almonds, walnuts)
- one tsp honey or maple syrup (optional)

Directions:

1. Inside your saucepot, raise the water to a boil. Include the washed brown rice and decrease the temp. to low.

2. Cover then simmer for around fifteen-twenty mins or till the rice is soft and the water is immersed.

3. Stir in the almond milk and ground cinnamon. Cook for an extra two-three mins till the porridge denses.

4. Take out from temp. then divide the porridge into two containers.

5. Top with diced apples and chopped nuts.

6. Drizzle using honey or maple syrup if anticipated.

7. Serve warm.

Per serving: Calories: 250 kcal; Fat: 6gm; Carbs: 45gm; Protein: 5gm

Fruit Salad with Mint and Lime Dressing

Preparation time: ten mins

Cooking time: zero mins

Servings: two

Ingredients:

- one teacup diced mixed fruits (e.g., watermelon, cantaloupe, pineapple, grapes)
- Juice of one lime
- one tbsp honey
- Fresh mint leaves for garnish

Directions:

1. Inside a container, combine the diced mixed fruits.

2. Inside your separate small container, whisk together the lime juice & honey to create the dressing.

3. Transfer the dressing across the fruit salad and toss carefully to cover the fruits uniformly.

4. Garnish with fresh mint leaves.

5. Serve cooled.

Per serving: Calories: 100 kcal; Fat: 0gm; Carbs: 25gm; Protein: 1gm

Smoothie Bowl with Kale and Mixed Berries

Preparation time: ten mins

Cooking time: zero mins

Servings: one

Ingredients:

- one teacup chopped kale leaves
- half teacup mixed berries (e.g., strawberries, blueberries, raspberries)
- half ripe banana
- half teacup almond milk (unsweetened)
- one tbsp chia seeds
- one tbsp honey or maple syrup (optional)
- Fresh fruit and nuts for topping (optional)

Directions:

1. In a blender, combine the chopped kale, mixed berries, banana, almond milk, and chia seeds.

2. Blend till uniform and creamy.

3. If the smoothie is too dense, place more almond milk to reach your anticipated uniformity.

4. Taste the smoothie and sweeten with honey or maple syrup if needed.

5. Pour the smoothie into a container.

6. Top with fresh fruit & nuts if anticipated.

7. Serve instantly.

Per serving: Calories: 250 kcal; Fat: 8gm; Carbs: 40gm; Protein: 6gm

Banana Walnut Muffins

Preparation time: fifteen mins

Cooking time: twenty mins

Servings: six

Ingredients:

- one teacup whole wheat flour
- one tsp baking powder
- half tsp baking soda
- quarter tsp salt
- two ripe bananas, mashed
- quarter teacup honey or maple syrup
- quarter teacup unsweetened applesauce
- quarter teacup almond milk (unsweetened)
- half tsp vanilla extract
- quarter teacup severed walnuts

Directions:

1. Warm up your oven to 350 deg. F then line a muffin tin using paper liners.

2. In a huge mixing container, blend the whole wheat flour, baking soda, baking powder, & salt.

3. Inside your distinct container, whisk collectively the mashed bananas, honey or maple syrup, unsweetened applesauce, almond milk, and vanilla extract till well combined.

4. Bring your wet components in to your dry components then carefully mix till just blended.

5. Wrap in the severed walnuts.

6. Put the batter into your muffin tin, stuffing each cup about two-thirds full.

7. Bake for approximately eighteen-twenty mins or 'til a toothpick immersed in the middle of your muffin comes out clean.

8. Let the muffins to cool mildly prior to serving.

Per serving: Calories: 180 kcal; Fat: 5gm; Carbs: 32gm; Protein: 4gm

Breakfast Burrito with Black Beans and Salsa

Preparation time: ten mins

Cooking time: ten mins

Servings: two

Ingredients:

- four whole-grain tortillas
- one teacup black beans (cooked or canned, that is drained and washed)
- one teacup cubed tomatoes
- half teacup cubed onions
- half teacup cubed bell peppers
- quarter teacup severed fresh cilantro
- Salt and pepper as required

Directions:

1. Inside a non-stick griddle, warm the black beans at middling temp. till warmed through. Flavor with salt and pepper as required.

2. Inside a separate griddle, sauté the cubed onions and bell peppers till they soften.

3. Warm the whole-grain tortillas in the microwave or oven.

4. Assemble your burritos by spreading a layer of black beans on each tortilla, followed by sautéed onions and bell peppers, cubed tomatoes, and severed fresh cilantro.

5. Wrap the sides of the tortillas then roll them up to form burritos.

6. Serve instantly.

Per serving: Calories: 300 kcal; Fat: 5gm; Carbs: 55gm; Protein: 10gm

Blueberry Almond Overnight Oats

Preparation time: five mins (plus overnight soaking)

Cooking time: zero mins

Servings: one

Ingredients:

- half teacup rolled oats
- half teacup almond milk (unsweetened)
- quarter teacup fresh blueberries
- one tbsp severed almonds
- one tsp honey or maple syrup (optional)

Directions:

1. Inside a jar or airtight container, blend the rolled oats and almond milk.

2. Include fresh blueberries and severed almonds to the solution.

3. Stir thoroughly to ensure all the components are blended.

4. Conceal the jar then refrigerate overnight or for at least 4 hours.

5. In the morning, give the overnight oats a good stir, and if anticipated, spray with honey or maple syrup for sweetness.

6. Serve cooled.

Per serving: Calories: 250 kcal; Fat: 8gm; Carbs: 35gm; Protein: 7gm

Veggie and Mushroom Scramble

Preparation time: ten mins

Cooking time: ten mins

Servings: two

Ingredients:

- four egg whites
- half teacup severed mixed vegetables (e.g., bell peppers, mushrooms, spinach)
- quarter teacup cubed tomatoes
- one tbsp severed fresh parsley
- Salt and pepper as required
- one tsp olive oil

Directions:

1. Inside your container, whisk the egg whites till frothy. Flavor with salt and pepper.

2. Inside your non-stick griddle, warm the olive oil at middling temp.

3. Include the severed mixed vegetables and sauté till they soften.

4. Include the cubed tomatoes then cook for an extra two-three mins.

5. Pour the whisked egg whites into your griddle with the vegetables.

6. Cook till the egg whites are set, stirring occasionally.

7. Spray your severed fresh parsley on top prior to serving.

Per serving: Calories: 100 kcal; Fat: 4gm; Carbs: 10gm; Protein: 10gm

Chapter 4. Juices and Smoothies

Green Detox Juice

Preparation time: ten mins

Cooking time: zero mins

Servings: one

Ingredients:

- one teacup kale leaves (stems removed)
- half cucumber
- two stalks celery
- half lemon (peeled)
- half teacup water

Directions:

1. Wash the entire components thoroughly.

2. Chop the cucumber, celery, and kale into smaller pieces.

3. Include the entire components into a mixer.

4. Blend 'til uniform and pour into a glass.

5. Serve instantly.

Per serving: Calories: 80 kcal; Fat: 0.5 gm; Carbs: 17 gm; Protein: 3 gm

Berry Blast Smoothie

Preparation time: five mins

Cooking time: zero mins

Servings: one

Ingredients:

- one teacup mixed berries (strawberries, blueberries, raspberries)
- one teacup spinach leaves
- one teacup unsweetened almond milk

Directions:

1. Wash the berries and spinach leaves.

2. Put the entire components in a mixer.

3. Blend till uniform and creamy.

4. Put into a glass, and then proceed with serving.

Per serving: Calories: 120 kcal; Fat: 3 gm; Carbs: 20 gm; Protein: 3 gm

Cucumber and Mint Cooler

Preparation time: five mins

Cooking time: zero mins

Servings: one

Ingredients:

- half cucumber
- quarter teacup fresh mint leaves
- one teacup water
- Ice cubes (optional)

Directions:

1. Peel and chop the cucumber into chunks.

2. Wash the mint leaves.

3. Place cucumber and mint in a mixer.

4. Include water and ice cubes if using.

5. Blend 'til uniform.

6. Transfer into your glass and garnish with a mint sprig.

7. Serve cooled.

Per serving: Calories: 15 kcal; Fat: 0 gm; Carbs: 3 gm; Protein: 1 gm

Carrot-Orange Juice

Preparation time: ten mins

Cooking time: zero mins

Servings: 1

Ingredients:

- two medium-sized carrots
- 1 large orange (peeled)
- half teacup water

Directions:

1. Wash and peel the carrots.

2. Peel the orange and take out any seeds.

3. Cut the carrots and orange into smaller pieces.

4. Place them in a mixer along with water.

5. Blend till uniform.

6. Put into a glass and enjoy.

Per serving: Calories: 80 kcal; Fat: 0.5 gm; Carbs: 18 gm; Protein: 1 gm

Beetroot and Apple Smoothie

Preparation time: seven mins

Cooking time: zero mins

Servings: one

Ingredients:

• one small beetroot (peeled and severed)

• one medium apple (cored and severed)

• half teacup unsweetened almond milk

• half tsp fresh ginger (grated)

• one tbsp lemon juice

• Ice cubes (optional)

Directions:

1. Wash and peel the beetroot. Chop it into smaller pieces.

2. Core and chop the apple.

3. Place the severed beetroot and apple in a mixer.

4. Include almond milk, grated ginger, and lemon juice.

5. Blend till uniform and creamy.

6. If anticipated, place a few ice cubes and blend again.

7. Transfer the smoothie into your glass and serve.

Per serving: Calories: 120 kcal; Fat: 2 gm; Carbs: 25 gm; Protein: 2 gm

Watermelon and Cucumber Slushie

Preparation time: five mins

Cooking time: zero mins

Servings: one

Ingredients:

• two teacups cubed watermelon (seeds removed)

• half cucumber

• one tbsp fresh lime juice

• Mint leaves for garnish (optional)

Directions:

1. Chop the watermelon and cucumber into chunks.

2. Place them in a mixer.

3. Include the fresh lime juice.

4. Blend till uniform.

5. Put the slushie into a glass and garnish with mint leaves if anticipated.

6. Serve instantly.

Per serving: Calories: 80 kcal; Fat: 0.5 gm; Carbs: 20 gm; Protein: 2 gm

Pineapple and Ginger Green Juice

Preparation time: eight mins

Cooking time: zero mins

Servings: one

Ingredients:

• one teacup severed pineapple

• one teacup spinach leaves

• half inch piece of fresh ginger

• half teacup water

Directions:

1. Peel then chop the ginger into small pieces.

2. Wash the pineapple and spinach leaves.

3. Put the entire components inside a mixer.

4. Mix till uniform and thoroughly blended.

5. Put the green juice into your glass and serve.

Per serving: Calories: 100 kcal; Fat: 0.5 gm; Carbs: 24 gm; Protein: 2 gm

Pomegranate and Blueberry Smoothie

Preparation time: five mins

Cooking time: zero mins

Servings: one

Ingredients:

- half teacup pomegranate seeds
- half teacup blueberries (fresh or frozen)
- one teacup unsweetened coconut water

Directions:

1. Combine pomegranate seeds, blueberries, and coconut water in a mixer.

2. Blend 'til uniform and creamy.

3. Put the smoothie into the glass of your choice and then relish it.

Per serving: Calories: 90 kcal; Fat: 0.5 gm; Carbs: 21 gm; Protcin: 2 gm

Cantaloupe and Ginger Juice

Preparation time: ten mins

Cooking time: zero mins

Servings: one

Ingredients:

- one teacup cubed cantaloupe
- half inch piece of fresh ginger
- half teacup water
- one tbsp fresh lime juice
- Ice cubes (optional)

Directions:

1. Peel then chop the ginger into small pieces.

2. Cut the cantaloupe into cubes.

3. Put the cantaloupe and ginger in a mixer.

4. Include water and fresh lime juice.

5. Blend till uniform and well mixed.

6. If anticipated, place a few ice cubes and blend again.

7. Transfer the juice into your glass and serve.

Per serving: Calories: 70 kcal; Fat: 0.5 gm; Carbs: 18 gm; Protein: 1 gm

Pear and Spinach Smoothie

Preparation time: seven mins

Cooking time: zero mins

Servings: one

Ingredients:

- one ripe pear (cored and severed)
- one teacup spinach leaves
- half teacup unsweetened almond milk
- one tbsp honey (optional, for sweetness)

Directions:

1. Wash and core the pear, then chop it into smaller pieces.

2. Wash the spinach leaves.

3. Put the severed pear and spinach in a mixer.

4. Include unsweetened almond milk.

5. If you prefer a sweeter taste, place a tablespoon of honey.

6. Blend till uniform and creamy.

7. Pour the smoothie into your glass then enjoy.

Per serving: Calories: 120 kcal; Fat: 2 gm; Carbs: 28 gm; Protein: 2 gm

Mango and Passion Fruit Smoothie

Preparation time: five mins

Cooking time: zero mins

Servings: one

Ingredients:

- one ripe mango (skinned and severed)
- Pulp from two passion fruits
- one teacup water

Directions:

1. Peel and chop the mango into chunks.

2. Scoop out the pulp from the passion fruits.

3. Put the mango and passion fruit pulp in a mixer.

4. Include water and blend till uniform.

5. Transfer the smoothie into your glass and serve.

Per serving: Calories: 130 kcal; Fat: 1 gm; Carbs: 32 gm; Protein: 2 gm

Mixed Fruit Medley Juice

Preparation time: ten mins

Cooking time: zero mins

Servings: one

Ingredients:

- half teacup mixed fruits (such as grapes, strawberries, kiwi, and orange segments)
- half teacup water
- one tbsp fresh lemon juice
- Ice cubes (optional)

Directions:

1. Wash and prepare the fruits (take out stems, peel, and chop if necessary).

2. Put the mixed fruits in a mixer.

3. Include water and fresh lemon juice.

4. Blend till uniform.

5. If anticipated, place a few ice cubes and blend again.

6. Transfer the juice into your glass and serve.

Per serving: Calories: 70 kcal; Fat: 0.5 gm; Carbs: 18 gm; Protein: 1 gm

Spinach and Kiwi Smoothie

Preparation time: five mins

Cooking time: zero mins

Servings: one

Ingredients:

- one teacup fresh spinach leaves
- two ripe kiwis (skinned and severed)
- half teacup unsweetened almond milk
- one tbsp honey (optional, for sweetness)

Directions:

1. Wash the spinach leaves thoroughly.

2. Peel and slice the kiwis into smaller parts.

3. Put the spinach and kiwi in a mixer.

4. Include unsweetened almond milk.

5. If you prefer a sweeter taste, place a tablespoon of honey.

6. Blend till uniform and creamy.

7. Put the smoothie into the glass of your choice and then relish it.

Per serving: Calories: 150 kcal; Fat: 2 gm; Carbs: 32 gm; Protein: 4 gm

Papaya and Lime Juice

Preparation time: seven mins

Cooking time: zero mins

Servings: one

Ingredients:

- one teacup ripe papaya (skinned and severed)
- Juice of one lime
- half teacup water
- one tbsp honey (optional, for sweetness)
- Ice cubes (optional)

Directions:

1. Peel and chop the papaya into chunks.

2. Squeeze the juice from the lime.

3. Put the papaya and lime juice in a mixer.

4. Include water and blend till uniform.

5. If anticipated, include honey for extra sweetness and ice cubes for a refreshing chill.

6. Blend again till well mixed.

7. Transfer the juice into your glass and serve.

Per serving: Calories: 120 kcal; Fat: 1 gm; Carbs: 30 gm; Protein: 2 gm

Tropical Smoothie

Preparation time: five mins

Cooking time: zero mins

Servings: one

Ingredients:

- one teacup severed pineapple
- one teacup severed ripe mango
- one teacup coconut water

Directions:

1. Peel and chop the pineapple and mango into chunks.

2. Put the severed fruits in a mixer.

3. Include coconut water.

4. Blend till uniform and creamy.

5. Put the smoothie into the glass of your choice and then relish the tropical flavors.

Per serving: Calories: 180 kcal; Fat: 1 gm; Carbs: 45 gm; Protein: 2 gm

Chapter 5. Lunch Recipes

Baked Salmon with Steamed Asparagus

Preparation time: ten mins

Cooking time: fifteen mins

Servings: two

Ingredients:

- two salmon fillets (six oz. each)
- one bunch of asparagus, clipped
- one tbsp olive oil
- Lemon slices for serving
- Fresh dill for garnish (optional)

Directions:

1. Warm up the oven to 400 deg.F.

2. Put the salmon fillets on a baking tray that has been covered in parchment paper before bringing them in.

3. Drizzle olive oil across the salmon then season with salt and pepper as required.

4. Arrange the clipped asparagus around the salmon onto the baking tray.

5. Bake in your warmed up oven for twelve-fifteen mins or 'til the salmon is cooked through and the asparagus is soft.

6. Serve the baked salmon and steamed asparagus with lemon slices and garnish with fresh dill if anticipated.

Per serving: Calories: 350 kcal; Fat: 20gm; Carbs: 5gm; Protein: 35gm

Stuffed Bell Peppers with Quinoa and Lentils

Preparation time: twenty mins

Cooking time: thirty mins

Servings: four

Ingredients:

- four big bell peppers (any color)
- half teacup cooked quinoa
- half teacup cooked lentils
- one teacup cubed tomatoes (no salt added)
- one teacup cubed zucchini
- half teacup cubed onion
- two pieces garlic, crushed
- one tsp dried oregano
- one tsp ground cumin
- Salt and pepper as required
- half teacup low-sodium vegetable broth
- quarter teacup shredded low-fat mozzarella cheese or dairy-free cheese (optional, for topping)

Directions:

1. Warm up the oven to 375 deg.F.

2. Take out the tops of the bell peppers, and subsequently slice open the peppers and removing the seeds and membranes.

3. In a large griddle, sauté the cubed onion and crushed garlic till the onion becomes luminous.

4. Include the cubed zucchini, cooked quinoa, cooked lentils, cubed tomatoes, dried oregano, ground cumin, salt, and pepper to the griddle, stirring to blend everything.

5. Pour the low-sodium vegetable broth into the griddle and let the solution simmer for a couple of mins till the flavors blend.

6. Stuff every bell pepper with the quinoa and lentil solution, packing it down mildly.

7. Put the stuffed bell peppers in your baking dish and cover with foil.

8. Bake in your warmed up oven for twenty to twenty-five mins or 'til the bell peppers are soft.

9. If using cheese, take out the foil and sprinkle your shredded cheese on top of each stuffed pepper, then bake for an extra five mins or till the cheese melts.

10. Serve the stuffed bell peppers hot.

Per serving: Calories: 250 kcal; Fat: 3gm; Carbs: 45gm; Protein: 15gm

Chickpea and Roasted Vegetable Bowl

Preparation time: fifteen mins

Cooking time: twenty-five mins

Servings: two

Ingredients:

• one tin (fifteen oz) chickpeas, that is drained and washed

• one teacup cubed sweet potatoes

• one teacup cubed bell peppers

• one teacup cubed zucchini

• one tbsp olive oil

• one tsp ground cumin

• half tsp smoked paprika

• Salt and pepper as required

• Mixed salad greens (lettuce, spinach, arugula, etc.)

• Lemon tahini dressing (low-fat or homemade)

Directions:

1. Warm up the oven to 425 deg.F.

2. Inside a big container, toss the cubed sweet potatoes, bell peppers, and zucchini with olive oil, ground cumin, smoked paprika, salt, and pepper till coated.

3. Distribute the vegetables in an even layer on a baking tray that has been covered with parchment paper.

4. Roast your vegetables in your warmed up oven for around twenty to twenty-five mins or till soft and mildly caramelized.

5. Inside a distinct container, blend the drained and washed chickpeas with a sprinkle of ground cumin and smoked paprika for extra flavor.

6. In serving containers, layer the mixed salad greens, roasted vegetables, and seasoned chickpeas.

7. Drizzle with lemon tahini dressing.

Per serving: Calories: 300 kcal; Fat: 10gm; Carbs: 45gm; Protein: 10gm

Brown Rice and Grilled Chicken Bowl

Preparation time: fifteen mins

Cooking time: twenty mins

Servings: two

Ingredients:

• one teacup cooked brown rice

• two boneless, skinless chicken breasts

• one teacup broccoli florets

• one teacup sliced bell peppers

• one tbsp olive oil

• one tsp garlic powder

• half tsp paprika

• Salt and pepper as required

• Lemon wedges for serving

Directions:

1. Cook the brown rice using the package instructions.

2. Warm up the grill or stovetop grill pan.

3. Flavor the chicken breasts using garlic powder, paprika, salt, and pepper.

4. Grill the chicken for around six-seven mins on all sides or till thoroughly cooked.

5. In a separate pan, sauté the broccoli florets and sliced bell peppers in olive oil till soft-crisp.

6. Split the cooked brown rice into two containers.

7. Slice the grilled chicken and place it on top of the rice in each container.

8. Include the sautéed broccoli and bell peppers to the containers.

9. Squeeze a lemon wedge over each container prior to serving.

Per serving: Calories: 400 kcal; Fat: 10g; Carbs: 40gm; Protein: 35g

Quinoa and Black Bean Salad

Preparation time: fifteen mins

Cooking time: fifteen mins

Servings: four

Ingredients:

• one teacup cooked quinoa

• one tin (fifteen oz) black beans, that is drained and washed

• one teacup cherry tomatoes, halved

• half teacup cubed cucumber

• quarter teacup severed fresh cilantro

• two tbsps lime juice

• one tbsp olive oil

• half tsp ground cumin

• Salt and pepper as required

• Avocado slices for serving (optional)

Directions:

1. Inside a big container, blend the cooked quinoa, black beans, cherry tomatoes, cubed cucumber, and severed cilantro.

2. Inside your distinct small container, whisk collectively the lime juice, olive oil, ground cumin, salt, and pepper to create the dressing.

3. Transfer the dressing across the quinoa and black bean solution, tossing everything together till well blended.

4. Split the salad into serving containers.

5. Top every serving with avocado slices, if anticipated.

Per serving: Calories: 300 kcal; Fat: 7gm; Carbs: 48g; Protein: 12g

Sautéed Spinach and Mushroom Quesadilla

Preparation time: ten mins

Cooking time: fifteen mins

Servings: two

Ingredients:

• four whole wheat tortillas (low-fat)

• two teacups fresh spinach leaves

• one teacup sliced mushrooms

• half teacup shredded low-fat mozzarella cheese or dairy-free cheese

• one tsp olive oil

• Salt and pepper as required

• Salsa or Greek yogurt (low-fat) for serving (optional)

Directions:

1. Inside your big griddle, warm the olive oil at middling temp.

2. Bring the sliced mushrooms to the griddle and sauté till they discharge their moisture and turn out to be soft.

3. Bring the fresh spinach leaves to the griddle and sauté till wilted.

4. Flavor the mushrooms and spinach with salt and pepper as required.

5. Take out the vegetables from the griddle then put away.

6. In the same griddle, place one tortilla and disperse half of the sautéed vegetables on top.

7. Spray half of the shredded cheese across the vegetables.

8. Top with another tortilla to create a quesadilla.

9. Cook the quesadilla for around two-three mins on all sides or till the tortillas are mildly browned and the cheese has melted.

10. Repeat the process to make the second quesadilla.

11. Slice each quesadilla into wedges then serve with salsa or Greek yogurt if anticipated.

Per serving: Calories: 300 kcal; Fat: 8gm; Carbs: 45gm; Protein: 15gm

Tofu Stir-Fry with Colorful Veggies

Preparation time: fifteen mins

Cooking time: ten mins

Servings: two

Ingredients:

• eight oz firm tofu, cubed

• one teacup broccoli florets

• one teacup sliced bell peppers

• one teacup sliced carrots

• one tbsp low-sodium soy sauce or tamari

• one tbsp hoisin sauce (look for one without added sugar)

• one tsp sesame oil

• one tsp cornstarch (optional, for thicker sauce)

• two green onions, sliced (for garnish)

Directions:

1. Inside a big non-stick pan or wok, warm the sesame oil at medium-high temp.

2. Bring the cubed tofu to the pot and cook 'til mildly browned and crispy on the edges.

3. Include the sliced bell peppers, broccoli florets, and carrots to the pan, stirring continuously.

4. Inside a small container, blend collectively the low-sodium soy sauce or tamari and hoisin sauce (and cornstarch if using) to make the sauce.

5. Put the sauce across the tofu and vegetables, stirring to cover everything uniformly.

6. Cook for a couple more mins till the sauce denses and the vegetables are soft-crisp.

7. Serve the tofu stir-fry over cooked brown rice or quinoa, if anticipated.

8. Garnish with sliced green onions.

Per serving: Calories: 280 kcal; Fat: 11gm; Carbs: 30gm; Protein: 18gm

Thai Shrimp Lettuce Wraps

Preparation time: twenty mins

Cooking time: ten mins

Servings: two

Ingredients:

• eight oz cooked shrimp, skinned and deveined

• one teacup shredded cabbage or coleslaw mix

• half teacup shredded carrots

• quarter teacup severed fresh cilantro

• two tbsps lime juice

• one tbsp fish sauce

• one tbsp natural peanut butter (unsweetened)

• one tsp grated fresh ginger

• one piece garlic, crushed

• Red pepper flakes (optional, for heat)

• eight big lettuce leaves (such as butter lettuce or romaine)

Directions:

1. Inside a container, blend the cooked shrimp, shredded cabbage, shredded carrots, and severed cilantro.

2. Inside your distinct small container, whisk collectively the lime juice, fish sauce (or soy sauce), peanut butter, grated ginger, crushed garlic, and red pepper flakes (if utilizing) to create the dressing.

3. Pour the dressing across the shrimp and vegetable solution, tossing everything together till thoroughly covered.

4. Wash and dry the lettuce leaves, using them as wraps to enclose the Thai shrimp stuffing.

5. Serve the lettuce wraps instantly.

Per serving: Calories: 240 kcal; Fat: 8gm; Carbs: 15gm; Protein: 27gm

Eggplant and Chickpea Curry

Preparation time: fifteen mins

Cooking time: twenty-five mins

Servings: four

Ingredients:

• one big eggplant, cubed

• one tin (fifteen oz) chickpeas, that is drained and washed

• one onion, finely severed

• two pieces garlic, crushed

• one tbsp grated fresh ginger

• one tin (fourteen oz) cubed tomatoes (that is no salt added)

• one teacup vegetable broth (low-sodium)

• one tbsp curry powder

• one tsp ground cumin

• half tsp turmeric powder

• quarter tsp cayenne pepper (optional, for heat)

• Salt and pepper as required

• Fresh cilantro for garnish

• Cooked brown rice or quinoa (optional, for serving)

Directions:

1. Inside a big griddle or pot, sauté the severed onion, garlic, and grated ginger till the onion becomes luminous.

2. Include the cubed eggplant to the griddle and cook for a couple of mins till it starts to soften.

3. Stir in the curry powder, ground cumin, turmeric powder, and cayenne pepper (if using), coating the vegetables with the spices.

4. Include your cubed tomatoes and vegetable broth to the griddle, stirring everything together.

5. Cover and simmer the curry for around fifteen mins or till the eggplant is soft and thoroughly cooked.

6. Include your chickpeas to the curry and cook for an extra five mins to heat them through.

7. Regulate the seasoning using salt and pepper as required.

8. Serve the eggplant and chickpea curry over cooked brown rice or quinoa, if anticipated.

9. Garnish with fresh cilantro prior to serving.

Per serving: Calories: 240 kcal; Fat: 4gm; Carbs: 42gm; Protein: 9gm

Turkey and Veggie Wrap with Whole Grain Tortilla

Preparation time: ten mins

Cooking time: five mins

Servings: two

Ingredients:

• four oz cooked turkey breast, finely cut

• two whole grain tortillas (low-fat)

• half teacup mixed salad greens (lettuce, spinach, arugula, etc.)

• half teacup shredded carrots

• quarter teacup sliced cucumber

• quarter teacup sliced bell peppers

• Hummus (low-fat) or a favorite low-fat dressing for spreading

Directions:

1. Lay out the whole grain tortillas on a clean surface.

2. Disperse a thin layer of hummus or your preferred low-fat dressing on each tortilla.

3. Arrange the sliced turkey breast, mixed salad greens, shredded carrots, sliced cucumber, and bell peppers uniformly on each tortilla.

4. Carefully roll up the tortillas, folding in the sides to create a wrap.

5. Slice the wraps in half if anticipated and serve instantly, or wrap them in your parchment paper for a portable meal.

Per serving: Calories: 250 kcal; Fat: 4gm; Carbs: 28gm; Protein: 24gm

Baked Cod with Lemon and Herbs

Preparation time: ten mins

Cooking time: fifteen mins

Servings: two

Ingredients:

• two cod fillets (six oz each)

• one lemon, finely cut

• Fresh herbs (dill, parsley, or thyme), severed

• Salt and pepper as required

• Olive oil (optional, for drizzling)

Directions:

1. Warm up the oven to 375 deg.F.

2. Bring the cod fillets onto a baking tray lined with parchment paper.

3. Flavor the fillets using salt and pepper as required.

4. Top each fillet with a few slices of lemon then a sprinkle of fresh herbs.

5. Pour a little olive oil over your fish, if anticipated.

6. Bake the cod fillets in your warmed up oven for around twelve-fifteen mins or 'til the fish is thoroughly cooked then flakes simply with a fork.

7. Serve the baked cod with lemon and herbs with a side of steamed broccoli or other non-starchy vegetables.

Per serving: Calories: 180 kcal; Fat: 2gm; Carbs: 1gm; Protein: 40gm

Sweet Potato and Black Bean Chili

Preparation time: fifteen mins

Cooking time: thirty mins

Servings: four

Ingredients:

• two medium sweet potatoes, skinned and cubed

• one tin (fifteen oz) black beans, that is drained and washed

• one tin (fourteen oz) cubed tomatoes (that is no salt added)

• one onion, severed

• two pieces garlic, crushed

• one tbsp chili powder

• one tsp ground cumin

• half tsp smoked paprika

• Salt and pepper as required

• Fresh cilantro for garnish

• Lime wedges for serving

Directions:

1. Inside a big pot, sauté the severed onion and crushed garlic till the onion turn out to be luminous.

2. Bring the cubed sweet potatoes to the pot and cook for a couple of mins 'til they begin to soften.

3. Stir in the chili powder, ground cumin, smoked paprika, salt, and pepper, coating the sweet potatoes with the spices.

4. Include the black beans and cubed tomatoes to the pot, stirring everything together.

5. Cover and simmer the chili for around twenty to twenty-five mins or till the sweet potatoes are soft and the flavors have melded.

6. Regulate the seasoning using salt and pepper as required.

7. Serve the sweet potato and black bean chili in containers, garnished with fresh cilantro.

8. Squeeze your lime wedge over each serving for a burst of citrusy flavor.

Per serving: Calories: 270 kcal; Fat: 1gm; Carbs: 55gm; Protein: 11gm

Grilled Chicken Salad with Mixed Greens

Preparation time: fifteen mins

Cooking time: fifteen mins

Servings: two

Ingredients:

- two boneless, skinless chicken breasts
- Mixed salad greens (lettuce, spinach, arugula, etc.)
- Cherry tomatoes, halved
- Cucumber, sliced
- Red onion, finely cut
- Balsamic vinegar dressing (low-fat or homemade)

Directions:

1. Warm up the grill or stovetop grill pan.

2. Flavor the chicken breasts using salt and pepper or your favorite herbs and spices.

3. Grill the chicken for around six-seven mins on all sides or till thoroughly cooked.

4. Allow the chicken to relax for a couple of mins prior to slicing it into strips.

5. Inside a big container, blend the mixed salad greens, cherry tomatoes, cucumber, and red onion.

6. Toss the salad with your preferred balsamic vinegar dressing.

7. Split the salad into two plates and top each with sliced grilled chicken.

8. Serve instantly.

Per serving: Calories: 350 kcal; Fat: 7gm; Carbs: 15gm; Protein: 50gm

Lentil and Vegetable Soup

Preparation time: ten mins

Cooking time: twenty-five mins

Servings: four

Ingredients:

- one teacup dried lentils, washed and drained
- one big carrot, cubed
- one celery stalk, cubed
- one small onion, scvered
- two pieces garlic, crushed
- four teacups vegetable broth (low-sodium)
- one bay leaf
- one tsp dried thyme
- Salt and pepper as required
- Fresh parsley for garnish

Directions:

1. Inside a big pot, sauté the severed onion, garlic, carrot, and celery in a little water or vegetable broth till softened.

2. Include the dried lentils, vegetable broth, salt, bay leaf, dried thyme, and pepper to the pot.

3. Boil the soup, then decrease the temp. to a simmer and cover.

4. Cook for around twenty to twenty-five mins or till the lentils are soft.

5. Take out the bay leaf then regulate the seasoning if required.

6. Serve the lentil and vegetable soup hot, garnished with fresh parsley.

Per serving: Calories: 250 kcal; Fat: 1gm; Carbs: 45gm; Protein: 15gm

Zucchini Noodles with Pesto Sauce

Preparation time: fifteen mins

Cooking time: five mins

Servings: two

Ingredients:

- two medium zucchinis, spiralized or finely cut
- one teacup fresh basil leaves
- quarter teacup pine nuts or walnuts
- one piece garlic, crushed
- two tbsps extra-virgin olive oil
- one tbsp lemon juice
- Salt and pepper as required
- Cherry tomatoes, halved (optional, for garnish)
- Grated Parmesan cheese (optional, for garnish)

Directions:

1. In your blending container, blend the fresh basil, pine nuts or walnuts, crushed garlic, olive oil, lemon juice, salt, and pepper.

2. Blend 'til you get a uniform pesto sauce. Include a little water if required to regulate the consistency.

3. In a non-stick pan, sauté the zucchini noodles for around two-three mins till they soften mildly.

4. Put the zucchini noodles with the pesto sauce 'til thoroughly covered.

5. Garnish using cherry tomatoes and grated Parmesan cheese, if anticipated.

6. Serve instantly.

Per serving: Calories: 220 kcal; Fat: 18gm; Carbs: 10gm; Protein: 5gm

Chapter 6. Meat Recipes

Baked Chicken Thighs with Rosemary and Lemon

Preparation time: ten mins

Cooking time: thirty mins

Servings: four

Ingredients:

- four bone-in, skinless chicken thighs
- two tbsps olive oil
- one tbsp fresh rosemary, severed
- Zest of one lemon
- two pieces garlic, crushed
- Salt and pepper as required

Directions:

1. Warm up the oven to 400 deg.F.

2. Inside a container, mix olive oil, severed rosemary, lemon zest, crushed garlic, salt, and pepper.

3. Rub the chicken thighs using the olive oil solution, ensuring they are thoroughly covered.

4. Bring the chicken thighs onto a baking tray covered with parchment paper.

5. Bake in your warmed up oven for twenty-five to thirty mins or 'til the chicken is thoroughly cooked and the skin is crispy.

6. Serve with a side of steamed vegetables or a fresh salad.

Per serving: Calories: 250 kcal; Fat: 14gm; Carbs: 0gm; Protein: 28gm

Baked Chicken Meatloaf with Spinach

Preparation time: fifteen mins

Cooking time: forty-five mins

Servings: four

Ingredients:

- one lb. ground chicken (or turkey)
- one teacup fresh spinach, severed
- half teacup grated zucchini
- quarter teacup grated carrot
- quarter teacup finely severed onion
- two pieces garlic, crushed
- quarter teacup whole wheat breadcrumbs
- one egg
- one tbsp Worcestershire sauce (optional)
- one tsp dried thyme
- Salt and pepper as required

Directions:

1. Warm up the oven to 375 deg.F.

2. Inside a big container, blend ground chicken, severed spinach, grated zucchini, grated carrot, severed onion, crushed garlic, breadcrumbs, egg, Worcestershire sauce (if using), dried thyme, salt, and pepper.

3. Mix everything till thoroughly blended.

4. Bring the solution to a loaf pan or shape it into a loaf on your baking tray lined with parchment paper.

5. Bake in your warmed up oven for forty to forty-five mins or 'til the meatloaf is thoroughly cooked and browned on top.

6. Allow it to relax for a couple of mins prior to slicing and serving.

Per serving: Calories: 200 kcal; Fat: 8gm; Carbs: 10gm; Protein: 24gm

Pork Stir-Fry with Bok Choy and Garlic

Preparation time: twenty mins

Cooking time: fifteen mins

Servings: four

Ingredients:

- one lb. pork tenderloin, finely cut
- four teacups bok choy, severed
- one red bell pepper, sliced
- one tbsp grated ginger
- three pieces garlic, crushed
- two tbsps low-sodium soy sauce
- one tbsp rice vinegar
- one tbsp hoisin sauce
- one tbsp cornstarch
- one tbsp vegetable oil

Directions:

1. In your small container, mix soy sauce, rice vinegar, hoisin sauce, and cornstarch to make the sauce.

2. Warm vegetable oil inside a huge griddle or wok at medium-high temp.

3. Include grated ginger and crushed garlic, stir-fry for a min till fragrant.

4. Include the sliced pork to the griddle and stir-fry till it's browned and thoroughly cooked.

5. Include severed bok choy and sliced red bell pepper to the griddle, stir-fry for an extra two-three mins till the vegetables are soft-crisp.

6. Transfer the sauce across the stir-fry and throw all collectively till thoroughly covered.

7. Serve hot with steamed brown rice or quinoa.

Per serving: Calories: 250 kcal; Fat: 10gm; Carbs: 10gm; Protein: 28gm

Grilled Game Meat Skewers with Zucchini and Cherry Tomatoes

Preparation time: twenty mins

Cooking time: fifteen mins

Servings: four

Ingredients:

- one lb. game meat (such as venison or bison), cut into cubes
- two zucchinis, cut into chunks
- one teacup cherry tomatoes
- two tbsps olive oil
- one tbsp balsamic vinegar
- one tsp dried rosemary
- one tsp dried thyme
- Salt and pepper as required

Directions:

1. Inside your container, mix olive oil, balsamic vinegar, dried rosemary, salt, dried thyme, and pepper to make a marinade.

2. Include the game meat cubes to the marinade and let them marinate for at least ten mins.

3. Thread the marinated meat, zucchinis, and cherry tomatoes onto skewers.

4. Grill the skewers on a warmed up grill or stovetop grill pan for around 10-12 minutes, turning occasionally, 'til the meat is cooked to your desired doneness and the vegetables are soft.

Per serving: Calories: 220 kcal; Fat: 10g; Carbs: 8g; Protein: 28g

Turkey and Vegetable Stir-Fry

Preparation time: twenty mins

Cooking time: fifteen mins

Servings: four

Ingredients:

- one lb. ground turkey
- two teacups mixed vegetables (broccoli, carrots, bell peppers, snap peas, etc.)
- one tbsp grated ginger
- three pieces garlic, crushed
- two tbsps low-sodium soy sauce
- one tbsp oyster sauce (optional)
- one tbsp cornstarch
- one tbsp vegetable oil

Directions:

1. In your small container, mix soy sauce, oyster sauce (if using), and cornstarch to make the sauce.

2. Warm vegetable oil inside a huge griddle or wok at medium-high temp.

3. Include grated ginger and crushed garlic, stir-fry for a minute till fragrant.

4. Include the ground turkey to the griddle and stir-fry till it's thoroughly cooked and browned.

5. Include the mixed vegetables to your griddle, stir-fry for an extra three-four mins 'til the vegetables are soft-crisp.

6. Transfer the sauce across the stir-fry and throw all collectively till thoroughly covered.

7. Serve hot with steamed brown rice or quinoa.

Per serving: Calories: 240 kcal; Fat: 10gm; Carbs: 12gm; Protein: 26gm

Baked Salmon with Dijon Mustard Glaze

Preparation time: ten mins

Cooking time: fifteen mins

Servings: four

Ingredients:

- four salmon fillets
- two tbsps Dijon mustard
- one tbsp honey
- one tbsp lemon juice
- one tsp dried dill
- Salt and pepper as required

Directions:

1. Warm up the oven to 400 deg.F.

2. Bring the salmon fillets on a baking dish.

3. Inside your small container, mix Dijon mustard, honey, salt, lemon juice, dried dill, and pepper to make the glaze.

4. Brush the glaze across the salmon fillets.

5. Bake in your warmed up oven for twelve-fifteen mins or 'til the salmon is thoroughly cooked then flakes simply with a fork.

6. Serve.

Per serving: Calories: 250 kcal; Fat: 10gm; Carbs: 5gm; Protein: 30gm

Herb-Marinated Grilled Pork Chops

Preparation time: fifteen mins

Cooking time: fifteen mins

Servings: four

Ingredients:

- four boneless pork chops
- two tbsps olive oil
- one tbsp severed fresh rosemary
- one tbsp severed fresh thyme
- two pieces garlic, crushed
- one tbsp lemon juice
- Salt and pepper as required

Directions:

1. Inside a container, mix olive oil, severed rosemary, severed thyme, crushed garlic, lemon juice, salt, and pepper to make the marinade.

2. Coat the pork chops using the marinade and let them marinate for almost ten mins.

3. Warm up the grill or stovetop grill pan.

4. Grill the pork chops for around six-seven mins on all sides or till they are thoroughly cooked and have grill marks.

5. Serve hot.

Per serving: Calories: 280 kcal; Fat: 12gm; Carbs: 0gm; Protein: 40gm

Lean Beef and Vegetable Stir-Fry

Preparation time: twenty mins

Cooking time: fifteen mins

Servings: four

Ingredients:

- one lb. lean beef (such as sirloin or flank), finely cut
- two teacups mixed vegetables (broccoli, carrots, bell peppers, snap peas, etc.)
- one tbsp grated ginger
- three pieces garlic, crushed
- two tbsps low-sodium soy sauce
- one tbsp oyster sauce (optional)
- one tbsp cornstarch
- one tbsp vegetable oil

Directions:

1. Inside your small container, mix soy sauce, oyster sauce (if using), and cornstarch to make the sauce.

2. Heat vegetable oil in a huge griddle or wok at medium-high temp.

3. Include grated ginger and crushed garlic, stir-fry for a minute till fragrant.

4. Bring the sliced beef to the griddle and stir-fry till it's browned and thoroughly cooked.

5. Include the mixed vegetables to your griddle, stir-fry for an extra three-four mins 'til the vegetables are soft-crisp.

6. Transfer the sauce across the stir-fry and throw all collectively till thoroughly covered.

7. Serve hot with steamed brown rice or quinoa.

Per serving: Calories: 280 kcal; Fat: 10gm; Carbs: 12gm; Protein: 36gm

Turkey Meatballs with Marinara Sauce

Preparation time: twenty mins

Cooking time: twenty-five mins

Servings: four

Ingredients:

- one lb. ground turkey
- quarter teacup whole wheat breadcrumbs
- quarter teacup grated Parmesan cheese
- one egg
- one tsp dried basil
- one tsp dried oregano
- half tsp garlic powder
- Salt and pepper as required
- two teacups low-sodium marinara sauce

Directions:

1. Warm up the oven to 375 deg.F.

2. Inside a container, mix ground turkey, breadcrumbs, grated Parmesan cheese, egg, dried basil, dried oregano, garlic powder, salt, and pepper till well blended.

3. Form the solution into meatballs then put them onto a baking tray covered using parchment paper.

4. Bake your meatballs in your warmed up oven for twenty to twenty-five mins or till thoroughly cooked.

5. Heat the marinara sauce in a saucepan.

6. Serve the turkey meatballs with the warm marinara sauce.

Per serving: Calories: 220 kcal; Fat: 8gm; Carbs: 15gm; Protein: 24gm

Baked Cod with Lemon and Dill

Preparation time: ten mins

Cooking time: fifteen mins

Servings: four

Ingredients:

- four cod fillets
- two tbsps olive oil
- one lemon, finely cut
- two tbsps fresh dill, severed
- Salt and pepper as required

Directions:

1. Warm up the oven to 400 deg.F.

2. Put the cod fillets on a baking dish.

3. Spray olive oil across the cod and flavor with salt and pepper.

4. Lay lemon slices on top of the fillets and spray with fresh dill.

5. Bake in your warmed up oven for twelve-fifteen mins or 'til the fish is cooked and flakes simply with a fork.

6. Serve.

Per serving: Calories: 180 kcal; Fat: 8gm; Carbs: 0gm; Protein: 25gm

Lean Beef Kebabs with Bell Peppers and Onions

Preparation time: twenty mins

Cooking time: fifteen mins

Servings: four

Ingredients:

- one lb. lean beef (such as sirloin), cut into cubes
- one red bell pepper, cut into chunks
- one yellow bell pepper, cut into chunks
- one red onion, cut into chunks
- two tbsps olive oil
- two tbsps balsamic vinegar
- one tsp dried thyme
- one tsp paprika
- Salt and pepper as required

Directions:

1. Inside your container, mix olive oil, balsamic vinegar, dried thyme, paprika, salt, and pepper to create a marinade.

2. Include the beef cubes to the marinade and let them marinate for almost ten mins.

3. Thread the marinated beef, bell peppers, and onions onto skewers.

4. Grill the kebabs on a warmed up grill or stovetop grill pan for around ten to twelve mins, turning occasionally, 'til the beef is cooked to your desired doneness and the vegetables are soft.

Per serving: Calories: 250 kcal; Fat: 12gm; Carbs: 10gm; Protein: 26gm

Steamed Fish with Ginger and Soy Sauce

Preparation time: ten mins

Cooking time: ten mins

Servings: four

Ingredients:

- one lb. white fish fillets (tilapia or cod)
- one inch piece of fresh ginger, finely cut
- three tbsps low-sodium soy sauce
- one tbsp rice vinegar
- one tbsp sesame oil
- two green onions, severed
- Steamed brown rice (optional, for serving)

Directions:

1. Prepare a steamer or a steaming basket with water and raise it to a boil.

2. Flavor the fish fillets using salt and place them on a heatproof plate.

3. Scatter the sliced ginger across the fish.

4. Inside your small container, mix soy sauce, rice vinegar, & sesame oil to create the sauce.

5. Pour the sauce across the fish and ginger.

6. Bring the plate in the steamer and cover with a lid. Steam the fish for around eight-ten mins or till it's fully cooked.

7. Put severed green onions on top prior to serving.

8. Serve with steamed brown rice, if anticipated.

Per serving: Calories: 180 kcal; Fat: 6gm; Carbs: 3gm; Protein: 26gm

Grilled Skinless Chicken Breast with Herbs

Preparation time: ten mins

Cooking time: fifteen mins

Servings: four

Ingredients:

- four skinless, boneless chicken breasts
- one tbsp olive oil
- one tsp dried thyme
- one tsp dried rosemary
- one tsp paprika
- Salt and pepper as required

Directions:

1. Warm up the grill or stovetop grill pan.

2. Inside a container, mix olive oil, thyme, rosemary, paprika, salt, and pepper to create a marinade.

3. Coat the chicken breasts using the marinade and let them sit for ten mins.

4. Grill the chicken breasts for around six-seven mins on all sides or till fully cooked.

5. Serve hot.

Per serving: Calories: 180 kcal; Fat: 6gm; Carbs: 0gm; Protein: 30gm

Baked Pork Tenderloin with Apple Chutney

Preparation time: fifteen mins

Cooking time: thirty mins

Servings: four

Ingredients:

- one lb. pork tenderloin
- two apples, skinned and cubed
- one small onion, finely severed
- one tbsp apple cider vinegar
- one tsp ground cinnamon
- one tsp ground ginger
- Salt and pepper as required

Directions:

1. Warm up the oven to 375 deg.F.

2. Flavor the pork tenderloin using salt and pepper and put it in a baking dish.

3. Inside a distinct container, mix cubed apples, severed onion, apple cider vinegar, ground cinnamon, ground ginger, salt, and pepper to create the chutney.

4. Disperse the apple chutney across the pork tenderloin.

5. Bake in your warmed up oven for twenty-five to thirty mins or 'til the pork is thoroughly cooked.

6. Allow it to relax for a couple of mins prior to slicing and serving.

Per serving: Calories: 240 kcal; Fat: 4gm; Carbs: 20gm; Protein: 28gm

Beef Stir-Fry with Broccoli and Snow Peas

Preparation time: fifteen mins

Cooking time: ten mins

Servings: four

Ingredients:

- one lb. lean beef (sirloin or flank), finely cut
- two teacups broccoli florets
- one teacup snow peas
- one red bell pepper, sliced
- two pieces garlic, crushed
- two tbsps low-sodium soy sauce
- one tbsp oyster sauce (optional)
- one tbsp cornstarch
- one tbsp vegetable oil

Directions:

1. Inside your small container, mix soy sauce, oyster sauce, and cornstarch to create the sauce.

2. Warm vegetable oil in a huge griddle or wok at medium-high temp.

3. Include crushed garlic and sliced beef, stir-fry till the beef is browned and thoroughly cooked.

4. Include broccoli, snow peas, and red bell pepper to the griddle, stir-fry for an extra three-four mins 'til the vegetables are soft-crisp.

5. Transfer the sauce across the stir-fry and throw all collectively till thoroughly covered.

6. Serve hot with steamed brown rice or quinoa.

Per serving: Calories: 280 kcal; Fat: 10gm; Carbs: 15gm; Protein: 30gm

Chapter 7. Fish Recipes

Baked Trout with Garlic and Olive Oil

Preparation time: ten mins

Cooking time: fifteen mins

Servings: two

Ingredients:

- two trout fillets
- three pieces garlic, crushed
- two tbsps olive oil
- one tbsp fresh lemon juice
- one tsp dried thyme
- one tsp paprika
- Salt and pepper as required

Directions:

1. Warm up the oven to 400 deg.F.

2. Put the trout fillets on your baking tray covered with parchment paper.

3. Inside your small container, blend collectively the crushed garlic, olive oil, lemon juice, dried thyme, paprika, salt, and pepper to create the marinade.

4. Pour the marinade across the trout fillets, ensuring they are uniformly covered.

5. Let the trout marinate for around five mins.

6. Bake the trout in your warmed up oven for around twelve-fifteen mins or till it's thoroughly cooked and simply flakes with a fork.

7. Serve the baked trout with a side of roasted vegetables and a fresh green salad.

Per serving: Calories: 250 kcal; Fat: 15gm; Carbs: 2gm; Protein: 30gm

Poached Salmon with Cucumber-Dill Sauce

Preparation time: fifteen mins

Cooking time: ten mins

Servings: two

Ingredients:

- two salmon fillets
- one cucumber, skinned and cubed
- quarter teacup plain Greek yogurt
- one tbsp fresh dill, severed
- one tbsp fresh lemon juice
- one tsp Dijon mustard
- Salt and pepper as required

Directions:

1. Fill a big griddle with sufficient water to across the salmon fillets. Bring the water to a gentle simmer in a middling temp.

2. Carefully place the salmon fillets in the simmering water. Poach the salmon for around 8-ten mins or till they are thoroughly cooked then flake simply with a fork.

3. While the salmon is poaching, prepare the cucumber-dill sauce. Inside your container, blend collectively the cubed cucumber, Greek yogurt, severed dill, lemon juice, Dijon mustard, salt, and pepper.

4. Once the salmon is done poaching, carefully take out the fillets from the water using a slotted spatula and place them on a plate.

5. Serve the poached salmon with a generous dollop of cucumber-dill sauce on top.

Per serving: Calories: 300 kcal; Fat: 15gm; Carbs: 6gm; Protein: 35gm

Baked Cod with Mediterranean Salsa

Preparation time: fifteen mins

Cooking time: fifteen mins

Servings: two

Ingredients:

- two cod fillets
- one teacup cherry tomatoes, halved
- quarter teacup pitted Kalamata olives, sliced
- two tbsps red onion, finely severed
- one tbsp fresh basil, severed
- one tbsp fresh parsley, severed
- one tbsp balsamic vinegar
- one tbsp olive oil
- Salt and pepper as required

Directions:

1. Warm up the oven to 375 deg.F.

2. Bring the cod fillets onto a baking tray covered with parchment paper.

3. Inside a container, blend collectively the halved cherry tomatoes, sliced Kalamata olives, severed red onion, severed basil, severed parsley, balsamic vinegar, olive oil, salt, and pepper to create the Mediterranean salsa.

4. Spoon the salsa across the cod fillets, covering them uniformly.

5. Bake the cod in your warmed up oven for around fifteen mins or till it's thoroughly cooked and flakes simply with a fork.

6. Serve the baked cod with a side of quinoa or couscous and a side salad.

Per serving: Calories: 250 kcal; Fat: 10gm; Carbs: 12gm; Protein: 30gm

Anchovy and Tomato Bruschetta

Preparation time: fifteen mins

Cooking time: seven mins

Servings: two

Ingredients:

- four slices whole-grain baguette or ciabatta
- four-six anchovy fillets, severed (regulate to your preference)
- one teacup cherry tomatoes, cubed
- one piece garlic, crushed
- one tbsp fresh basil, severed
- one tbsp balsamic vinegar
- one tbsp olive oil
- Salt and pepper as required

Directions:

1. Warm up the oven to 375 deg.F.

2. Put the slices of whole-grain baguette or ciabatta onto a baking tray.

3. Bring the bread slices in the warmed up oven for around five-seven mins or till they are mildly crisp and golden.

4. Inside a container, blend the severed anchovy fillets, cubed cherry tomatoes, crushed garlic, balsamic vinegar, severed basil, salt, olive oil, and pepper to create the bruschetta topping.

5. Spoon the anchovy and tomato solution across the toasted bread slices.

6. Serve the anchovy and tomato bruschetta as a delicious appetizer or a light lunch option.

Per serving: Calories: 200 kcal; Fat: 8gm; Carbs: 25gm; Protein: 8gm

Lemon Garlic Shrimp Scampi

Preparation time: ten mins

Cooking time: ten mins

Servings: two

Ingredients:

- one lb. medium shrimp, skinned and deveined
- three pieces garlic, crushed
- Zest and juice of one lemon
- two tbsps olive oil
- two tbsps fresh parsley, severed
- Salt and pepper as required
- Crushed red pepper flakes (optional)

Directions:

1. Inside a container, blend the crushed garlic, lemon zest, lemon juice, olive oil, severed parsley, pepper, salt, & crushed red pepper flakes (if using).

2. Bring the skinned and deveined shrimp to the container and toss them in the marinade. Let them marinate for around five-ten mins.

3. Heat your non-stick griddle at medium-high temp. and include the marinated shrimp to the pan. Cook for around two-three mins on all sides till they turn pink and opaque.

4. Serve the lemon garlic shrimp scampi with a side of quinoa or whole-grain pasta and steamed broccoli.

Per serving: Calories: 250 kcal; Fat: 10gm; Carbs: 10gm; Protein: 30gm

Sardine and Tomato Salad

Preparation time: ten mins

Cooking time: zero mins

Servings: two

Ingredients:

- one tin sardines in water, drained
- one teacup cherry tomatoes, halved
- quarter teacup red onion, finely cut
- one tbsp fresh basil, severed
- one tbsp balsamic vinegar
- one tbsp olive oil
- Salt and pepper as required

Directions:

1. Inside a container, carefully blend the drained sardines, finely cut red onion, halved cherry tomatoes, and severed basil.

2. Inside your distinct small container, whisk collectively the salt, balsamic vinegar, olive oil, and pepper to create the dressing.

3. Pour the dressing across the sardine and tomato solution then toss carefully to coat all components.

4. Let the flavors meld for a couple of mins prior to serving.

Per serving: Calories: 200 kcal; Fat: 10gm; Carbs: 6gm; Protein: 20gm

Grilled Mackerel with Lime and Cilantro

Preparation time: ten mins

Cooking time: ten mins

Servings: two

Ingredients:

- two mackerel fillets
- Juice and zest of one lime
- two tbsps fresh cilantro, severed
- one tbsp olive oil
- Salt and pepper as required

Directions:

1. Warm up the grill to medium-high temp.

2. Inside your container, blend collectively your lime juice, lime zest, severed cilantro, olive oil, salt, and pepper.

3. Rub your solution over both sides of the mackerel fillets.

4. Grill the mackerel for around four to five mins on all sides or till it's thoroughly cooked and has nice grill marks.

5. Serve the grilled mackerel with a side of quinoa or brown rice and steamed vegetables.

Per serving: Calories: 250 kcal; Fat: 15gm; Carbs: 1gm; Protein: 25gm

Baked Haddock with Herbed Bread Crumbs

Preparation time: fifteen mins

Cooking time: twenty mins

Servings: two

Ingredients:

- two haddock fillets
- quarter teacup whole wheat breadcrumbs
- one tbsp fresh parsley, severed
- one tbsp fresh thyme leaves
- one tbsp fresh lemon juice
- one tbsp olive oil
- Salt and pepper as required

Directions:

1. Warm up the oven to 375 deg.F.

2. Bring the haddock fillets onto a baking tray covered with parchment paper.

3. Inside a small container, blend collectively the breadcrumbs, severed parsley, thyme leaves, lemon juice, olive oil, salt, and pepper.

4. Press the herbed breadcrumb solution on top of each haddock fillet to form a crust.

5. Bake the haddock in your warmed up oven for around fifteen-twenty mins or till it's thoroughly cooked and the breadcrumbs are golden brown.

6. Serve the baked haddock with a side of roasted sweet potatoes then a mixed green salad.

Per serving: Calories: 200 kcal; Fat: 8gm; Carbs: 10gm; Protein: 25gm

Baked Snapper with Tomatoes and Olives

Preparation time: fifteen mins

Cooking time: twenty mins

Servings: two

Ingredients:

- two snapper fillets
- one teacup cherry tomatoes, halved
- quarter teacup black olives, that is pitted and sliced
- two pieces garlic, crushed
- one tbsp fresh basil, severed
- one tbsp fresh parsley, severed
- one tbsp olive oil
- Salt and pepper as required

Directions:

1. Warm up the oven to 375 deg.F.

2. Put the snapper fillets on your baking tray covered with parchment paper.

3. Inside a container, blend collectively the halved cherry tomatoes, black olives, crushed garlic, severed basil, severed parsley, olive oil, salt, and pepper.

4. Spoon the tomato & olive solution across the snapper fillets, covering them uniformly.

5. Bake in to your warmed up oven for fifteen-twenty mins or till the fish is cooked and simply flakes with a fork.

6. Serve the baked snapper with a side of steamed vegetables or a light salad.

Per serving: Calories: 250 kcal; Fat: 10gm; Carbs: 6gm; Protein: 35gm

Miso-Glazed Black Cod

Preparation time: ten mins

Cooking time: ten mins

Servings: two

Ingredients:

- two black cod fillets
- two tbsps white miso paste
- one tbsp mirin (Japanese sweet rice wine)
- one tbsp low-sodium soy sauce
- one tbsp rice vinegar
- one tsp grated ginger
- one tsp honey
- one green onion, finely cut (for garnish)

Directions:

1. Inside your container, whisk collectively the miso paste, mirin, soy sauce, rice vinegar, grated ginger, and honey to create the miso glaze.

2. Pat the black cod fillets dry with paper towels then place them in a shallow dish.

3. Pour the miso glaze across the fish, ensuring it coats all sides. Let it marinate in the fridge for around thirty mins.

4. Warm up the oven to 400 deg.F.

5. Take out the fish from the marinade then place it onto a baking tray covered using parchment paper.

6. Bake the black cod in the warmed up oven for around eight-ten mins or 'til the fish is cooked then flakes simply with a fork.

7. Garnish with finely cut green onions prior to serving.

Per serving: Calories: 300 kcal; Fat: 10gm; Carbs: 10gm; Protein: 40gm

Grilled Halibut with Mango Salsa

Preparation time: fifteen mins

Cooking time: ten mins

Servings: two

Ingredients:

- two halibut fillets
- one tbsp olive oil
- Salt and pepper as required
- For the Mango Salsa:
- one ripe mango, skinned and cubed
- one small red bell pepper, cubed
- quarter teacup red onion, finely severed
- one jalapeño pepper, seeds removed and finely severed (optional, regulate to your spice preference)
- one tbsp fresh cilantro, severed
- Juice of one lime
- Salt as required

Directions:

1. Warm up the grill to medium-high temp.

2. Rub the halibut fillets with olive oil and flavor them with salt and pepper.

3. Grill the halibut for around four to five mins on all sides or till it's thoroughly cooked and simply flakes with a fork.

4. Whilst the halibut is grilling, prepare the mango salsa by mixing all your salsa components in your container. Mix thoroughly then regulate the seasoning as required.

5. Once the halibut is done, serve it with a generous spoonful your mango salsa on top.

Per serving: Calories: 300 kcal; Fat: 10gm; Carbs: 20gm; Protein: 35gm

Seared Scallops with Citrus Dressing

Preparation time: ten mins

Cooking time: five mins

Servings: two

Ingredients:

- ten-twelve big sea scallops
- one tbsp olive oil
- Salt and pepper as required
- For the Citrus Dressing:
- Juice of one orange
- Juice of one lemon
- one tbsp olive oil
- one tsp Dijon mustard
- one piece garlic, crushed
- Salt and pepper as required

Directions:

1. Pat the scallops dry using paper towels to take out any extra moisture.

2. Flavor the scallops with salt and pepper.

3. In your non-stick griddle, warm the olive oil at medium-high temp.

4. Include the scallops to your griddle and sear them for around one-two mins on all sides till they are golden brown and thoroughly cooked.

5. While the scallops are cooking, prepare the citrus dressing by whisking together all your dressing components in your small container.

6. Once the scallops are done, spray the citrus dressing across them, and serve instantly.

Per serving: Calories: 200 kcal; Fat: 10gm; Carbs: 8gm; Protein: 20gm

Baked Salmon with Lemon and Herbs

Preparation time: ten mins

Cooking time: twenty mins

Servings: two

Ingredients:

- two salmon fillets
- one lemon, finely cut
- two tbsps fresh herbs (dill, parsley, or thyme), severed
- Salt and pepper as required

Directions:

1. Warm up the oven to 375 deg.F.

2. Put the salmon fillets on a baking tray that has been covered in parchment paper prior to bringing them in.

3. Flavor the salmon with salt and pepper.

4. Top each fillet with lemon slices and spray severed herbs across them.

5. Bake your salmon in your warmed up oven for around fifteen-twenty mins or till it's thoroughly cooked and flakes simply with a fork.

6. Serve warm and relish!

Per serving: Calories: 250 kcal; Fat: 12gm; Carbs: 2gm; Protein: 30gm

Tuna and Avocado Salad

Preparation time: fifteen mins

Cooking time: zero mins

Servings: two

Ingredients:

- one tin tuna (in water), drained
- one ripe avocado, cubed
- one cucumber, cubed
- one small red onion, finely severed
- one tbsp fresh cilantro, severed
- one tbsp olive oil
- Juice of one lime
- Salt and pepper as required

Directions:

1. Inside your blending container, blend the drained tuna, cubed avocado, cucumber, red onion, and severed cilantro.

2. Spray olive oil & lime juice across the salad.

3. Flavor using salt and pepper, and carefully throw all collectively.

4. Chill the salad in the refrigerator for almost fifteen mins prior to serving.

Per serving: Calories: 300 kcal; Fat: 20gm; Carbs: 10gm; Protein: 20gm

Lemon Pepper Tilapia

Preparation time: five mins

Cooking time: ten mins

Servings: two

Ingredients:

- two tilapia fillets
- one tbsp olive oil
- Zest of one lemon
- one tsp black pepper
- Salt as required

Directions:

1. Inside your container, blend collectively the olive oil, black pepper, lemon zest, & a tweak of salt.

2. Rub the solution over both sides of the tilapia fillets.

3. Heat your non-stick griddle at middling temp. and mildly oil it with olive oil.

4. Cook your tilapia fillets for around four to five mins on all sides or till they are thoroughly cooked and simply flake with a fork.

5. Serve the tilapia with a side of vegetables or salad.

Per serving: Calories: 200 kcal; Fat: 8gm; Carbs: 1gm; Protein: 30gm

Chapter 8. Salads and Sides Recipes

Mixed Green Salad with Balsamic Vinaigrette

Preparation time: ten mins

Cooking time: zero mins

Servings: two

Ingredients:

• four teacups mixed greens (spinach, arugula, lettuce, etc.)

• half teacup cherry tomatoes, halved

• quarter teacup cucumber, sliced

• quarter teacup red bell pepper, cubed

• quarter teacup red onion, finely cut

• two tbsps balsamic vinegar

• one tbsp extra-virgin olive oil

• one tsp Dijon mustard

• Salt and pepper as required

Directions:

1. Inside a big container, blend the mixed greens, cherry tomatoes, cucumber, red bell pepper, and red onion.

2. Inside your distinct small container, whisk collectively the balsamic vinegar, olive oil, Dijon mustard, salt, and pepper to create the dressing.

3. Spray your dressing across the salad then toss carefully to cover the greens uniformly.

4. Split the salad between two plates then serve instantly.

Per serving: Calories: 120 kcal; Fat: 7gm; Carbs: 12gm; Protein: 2gm

Quinoa and Roasted Vegetable Salad

Preparation time: fifteen mins

Cooking time: twenty-five mins

Servings: four

Ingredients:

• one teacup quinoa, washed

• two teacups water

• one medium zucchini, cubed

• one medium yellow bell pepper, cubed

• one teacup cherry tomatoes, halved

• one tbsp olive oil

• one tsp dried oregano

• half tsp garlic powder

• Salt and pepper as required

• two tbsps fresh lemon juice

• two tbsps severed fresh parsley

Directions:

1. Warm up your oven to 390 deg.F.

2. Inside your saucepot, bring the quinoa and water to a boil. Lower the temp., cover, then simmer for around fifteen mins or 'til the quinoa is cooked and the water is immersed.

3. While the quinoa is cooking, place the cubed zucchini, yellow bell pepper, and cherry tomatoes onto a baking tray. Spray with olive oil, spray using dried oregano, garlic powder, salt, and pepper. Toss to cover the vegetables uniformly.

4. Roast the vegetables in the warmed up oven for around twenty to twenty-five mins or till they are soft and mildly browned.

5. Inside a big container, blend the cooked quinoa and roasted vegetables. Spray using fresh lemon juice and spray with severed fresh parsley. Toss carefully to blend.

6. Serve the quinoa and roasted vegetable salad warm or at room temp.

Per serving: Calories: 230 kcal; Fat: 7gm; Carbs: 35gm; Protein: 8gm

Greek Cucumber and Tomato Salad

Preparation time: ten mins

Cooking time: zero mins

Servings: four

Ingredients:

• two big cucumbers, cubed

• two teacups cherry tomatoes, halved

• half red onion, finely cut

• half teacup Kalamata olives, that is pitted and halved

• quarter teacup crumbled feta cheese (optional, omit for a completely dairy-free version)

• two tbsps extra-virgin olive oil

• one tbsp red wine vinegar

• one tsp dried oregano

• Salt and pepper as required

Directions:

1. Inside a big container, blend the cubed cucumbers, cherry tomatoes, red onion, Kalamata olives, and crumbled feta cheese (if using).

2. Inside your small container, whisk collectively the extra-virgin olive oil, salt, red wine vinegar, dried oregano, and pepper to create the dressing.

3. Spray the dressing across the cucumber and tomato solution. Toss carefully to blend then cover the salad with the dressing.

4. Serve the Greek cucumber and tomato salad instantly or you can refrigerate for a couple of hrs to allow the flavors blend collectively.

Per serving: Calories: 160 kcal; Fat: 12gm; Carbs: 10gm; Protein: 4gm

Grilled Zucchini with Lemon and Herbs

Preparation time: ten mins

Cooking time: ten mins

Servings: four

Ingredients:

• two medium zucchinis, sliced lengthwise into quarter inch dense strips

• two tbsps extra-virgin olive oil

• one tbsp fresh lemon juice

• one tsp dried thyme

• one tsp dried rosemary

• Salt and pepper as required

Directions:

1. Warm up your grill or your stovetop grill pot at medium-high temp.

2. Inside a big container, toss the zucchini strips with extra-virgin olive oil, fresh lemon juice, dried thyme, dried rosemary, salt, and pepper.

3. Grill the zucchini strips for around three-five mins on all sides or till they have grill marks and are soft.

4. Take out the grilled zucchini from the heat and transfer to a serving platter.

5. Serve the grilled zucchini with lemon and herbs as a delicious and healthy side dish.

Per serving: Calories: 80 kcal; Fat: 7gm; Carbs: 4gm; Protein: 1gm

Roasted Brussels Sprouts with Garlic and Lemon

Preparation time: ten mins

Cooking time: twenty mins

Servings: four

Ingredients:

- one lb. Brussels sprouts, clipped and halved
- two tbsps extra-virgin olive oil
- two pieces garlic, crushed
- one tbsp fresh lemon juice
- Zest of one lemon
- Salt and pepper as required

Directions:

1. Warm up your oven to 390 deg.F.

2. Inside a big container, toss the halved Brussels sprouts with extra-virgin olive oil, crushed garlic, fresh lemon juice, lemon zest, salt, and pepper.

3. Disperse your Brussels sprouts in a single layer on your baking tray.

4. Roast the Brussels sprouts in the warmed up oven for around twenty mins or till they are golden brown and crispy on the edges.

5. Bring the roasted Brussels sprouts to a serving dish and serve as a flavorful and nutritious side dish.

Per serving: Calories: 100 kcal; Fat: 7gm; Carbs: 8gm; Protein: 3gm

Cabbage and Carrot Slaw with Apple Cider Vinegar Dressing

Preparation time: fifteen mins

Cooking time: zero mins

Servings: four

Ingredients:

- three teacups shredded green cabbage
- one teacup shredded carrots
- quarter teacup severed fresh parsley
- two tbsps apple cider vinegar
- one tbsp extra-virgin olive oil
- one tsp honey (optional, for a touch of sweetness)
- Salt and pepper as required

Directions:

1. Inside a big container, blend the shredded green cabbage, shredded carrots, and severed fresh parsley.

2. Inside your small container, whisk collectively the apple cider vinegar, extra-virgin olive oil, honey (if using), salt, and pepper to create the dressing.

3. Spray the dressing across the cabbage and carrot solution. Toss carefully to blend and cover the slaw with the dressing.

4. Let the slaw sit for a couple of mins prior to serving to allow the flavors to blend collectively.

5. Serve the cabbage and carrot slaw as a refreshing and crunchy side dish.

Per serving: Calories: 70 kcal; Fat: 4gm; Carbs: 8gm; Protein: 1gm

Steamed Asparagus with Lemon Zest

Preparation time: five mins

Cooking time: five mins

Servings: four

Ingredients:

• one bunch asparagus, tough ends clipped

• Zest of one lemon

• one tbsp extra-virgin olive oil

• Salt and pepper as required

Directions:

1. Boil a pot of water. Put a steamer basket across the pot.

2. Include the clipped asparagus to the steamer basket, cover, then steam for around four to five mins or till the asparagus is soft-crisp.

3. Take out the steamed asparagus from the basket and transfer to a serving platter.

4. Spray extra-virgin olive oil across the asparagus, spray with lemon zest, salt, and pepper.

5. Toss carefully to cover the asparagus using the flavors.

6. Serve the steamed asparagus with lemon zest as a nutritious and vibrant side dish.

Per serving: Calories: 40 kcal; Fat: 3gm; Carbs: 3gm; Protein: 2gm

Edamame and Avocado Salad

Preparation time: ten mins

Cooking time: zero mins

Servings: four

Ingredients:

• one teacup frozen edamame, thawed

• one ripe avocado, cubed

• quarter teacup severed fresh cilantro

• two tbsps lime juice

• one tbsp sesame oil

• one tbsp low-sodium soy sauce

• one tsp sesame seeds

• Salt and pepper as required

Directions:

1. Inside a big container, blend the thawed edamame, cubed avocado, and severed fresh cilantro.

2. Inside your distinct small container, whisk collectively the lime juice, sesame oil, salt, low-sodium soy sauce, sesame seeds, and pepper to create the dressing.

3. Spray the dressing across the edamame and avocado solution. Toss carefully to blend then cover the salad with the dressing.

4. Serve the edamame and avocado salad as a protein-rich and creamy side dish.

Per serving: Calories: 160 kcal; Fat: 12gm; Carbs: 10gm; Protein: 6gm

Tomato and Basil Caprese Salad

Preparation time: ten mins

Cooking time: zero mins

Servings: four

Ingredients:

• two big ripe tomatoes, sliced

• one ball fresh mozzarella cheese, sliced

• Fresh basil leaves

• two tbsps balsamic vinegar reduction (or balsamic glaze)

• one tbsp extra-virgin olive oil

• Salt and pepper as required

Directions:

1. On a serving platter, alternate the slices of tomatoes and fresh mozzarella.

2. Tuck fresh basil leaves between the tomato & mozzarella slices.

3. Spray balsamic vinegar reduction and extra-virgin olive oil across the Caprese salad.

4. Spray with salt and pepper as required.

5. Serve the Tomato and Basil Caprese Salad as a classic and delightful side dish.

Per serving: Calories: 180 kcal; Fat: 13gm; Carbs: 8gm; Protein: 9gm

Roasted Sweet Potato Wedges

Preparation time: ten mins

Cooking time: thirty mins

Servings: four

Ingredients:

• two big sweet potatoes, skinned then cut into wedges

• two tbsps olive oil

• one tsp paprika

• half tsp garlic powder

• half tsp onion powder

• Salt and pepper as required

Directions:

1. Warm up your oven to 390 deg.F.

2. Inside a big container, toss the sweet potato wedges with olive oil, paprika, garlic powder, onion powder, salt, and pepper till thoroughly covered.

3. Disperse your sweet potato wedges in a single layer on your baking tray.

4. Roast the sweet potato wedges in the warmed up oven for around twenty-five to thirty mins or till they are soft and mildly browned, flipping them halfway through cooking.

5. Serve the roasted sweet potato wedges as a delicious and nourishing side dish.

Per serving: Calories: 160 kcal; Fat: 7gm; Carbs: 23gm; Protein: 2gm

Chickpea and Cucumber Salad

Preparation time: ten mins

Cooking time: zero mins

Servings: four

Ingredients:

• one tin (fifteen oz) chickpeas (garbanzo beans), drained and washed

• one big cucumber, cubed

• quarter teacup cubed red onion

• quarter teacup severed fresh parsley

• two tbsps lemon juice

• two tbsps extra-virgin olive oil

• one tsp ground cumin

• Salt and pepper as required

Directions:

1. Inside a big container, blend the chickpeas, cubed cucumber, cubed red onion, and severed fresh parsley.

2. Inside your distinct small container, whisk collectively the lemon juice, extra-virgin olive oil, ground cumin, salt, and pepper to create the dressing.

3. Spray the dressing across the chickpea and cucumber solution. Toss carefully to blend then cover the salad with the dressing.

4. Let the chickpea and cucumber salad sit for a couple of mins prior to serving to allow the flavors to blend collectively.

5. Serve the chickpea and cucumber salad as a refreshing and protein-packed side dish.

Per serving: Calories: 180 kcal; Fat: 10gm; Carbs: 18gm; Protein: 6gm

Grilled Eggplant with Tahini Dressing

Preparation time: ten mins

Cooking time: ten mins

Servings: four

Ingredients:

• one big eggplant, sliced into rounds or lengthwise

• two tbsps olive oil

• two tbsps tahini (sesame seed paste)

• one tbsp lemon juice

• one piece garlic, crushed

• one tbsp water

• Fresh parsley for garnish (optional)

• Salt and pepper as required

Directions:

1. Warm up your grill or your stovetop grill pot at medium-high temp.

2. Brush both sides of your eggplant slices using olive oil and flavor using salt and pepper.

3. Grill the eggplant slices for around three-five mins on all sides or till they have grill marks and are soft.

4. Inside your small container, whisk collectively tahini, lemon juice, crushed garlic, water, salt, and pepper to create the dressing.

5. Arrange the grilled eggplant slices on your serving platter, spray with tahini dressing, and garnish with fresh parsley if anticipated.

6. Serve the Grilled Eggplant with Tahini Dressing as a tasty and nutritious side dish.

Per serving: Calories: 120 kcal; Fat: 9gm; Carbs: 9gm; Protein: 2gm

Spinach and Strawberry Salad with Balsamic Glaze

Preparation time: ten mins

Cooking time: zero mins

Servings: four

Ingredients:

• four teacups fresh baby spinach

• one teacup fresh strawberries, sliced

• quarter teacup sliced almonds

• two tbsps balsamic glaze

• one tbsp extra-virgin olive oil

• Salt and pepper as required

Directions:

1. Inside a big container, blend the fresh baby spinach, sliced strawberries, and sliced almonds.

2. Spray balsamic glaze and extra-virgin olive oil across the salad.

3. Toss carefully to blend then cover the salad with the dressing.

4. Flavor with salt and pepper as required.

5. Serve the Spinach and Strawberry Salad with Balsamic Glaze as a delightful and nutritious side dish.

Per serving: Calories: 120 kcal; Fat: 8gm; Carbs: 10gm; Protein: 3gm

Cauliflower Rice with Herbs and Lemon

Preparation time: ten mins

Cooking time: ten mins

Servings: four

Ingredients:

- one medium cauliflower head, florets only
- two tbsps extra-virgin olive oil
- two pieces garlic, crushed
- quarter teacup severed fresh parsley
- Zest of one lemon
- Salt and pepper as required

Directions:

1. In your blending container, pulse the cauliflower florets till they resemble rice-like grains.

2. Inside a big griddle, heat the extra-virgin olive oil at middling temp.

3. Include the crushed garlic and sauté for around one min till fragrant.

4. Include the cauliflower rice to the griddle and cook for around five-seven mins or till the cauliflower is soft, stirring occasionally.

5. Stir in the severed fresh parsley and lemon zest. Flavor with salt and pepper as required.

6. Serve the Cauliflower Rice with Herbs and Lemon as a flavorful and low-carb side dish.

Per serving: Calories: 90 kcal; Fat: 7gm; Carbs: 7gm; Protein: 3gm

Steamed Broccoli with Almonds

Preparation time: ten mins

Cooking time: five mins

Servings: four

Ingredients:

- one lb. broccoli florets
- two tbsps sliced almonds
- one tbsp extra-virgin olive oil
- one tbsp lemon juice
- Salt and pepper as required

Directions:

1. Boil a pot of water. Put a steamer basket across the pot.

2. Put the broccoli florets to the steamer basket, cover, then steam for around four to five mins or till the broccoli is soft-crisp.

3. In your small pan, toast the sliced almonds at middling temp. 'til mildly browned and fragrant. Keep your eye on them as they can burn simply.

4. Inside a big container, toss the steamed broccoli with extra-virgin olive oil, salt, lemon juice, and pepper.

5. Sprinkle the toasted sliced almonds across the broccoli.

6. Serve the Steamed Broccoli with Almonds as a nutritious and crunchy side dish.

Per serving: Calories: 80 kcal; Fat: 6gm; Carbs: 6gm; Protein: 3gm

Chapter 9. Dinner Recipes

Lemon Herb Baked Chicken Breast

Preparation time: ten mins

Cooking time: twenty-five mins

Servings: four

Ingredients:

• four boneless, skinless chicken breasts

• Juice of one lemon

• two tbsps olive oil

• one tsp dried thyme

• one tsp dried rosemary

• one tsp dried oregano

• Salt and pepper as required

Directions:

1. Warm up the oven to 375 deg.F.

2. Inside your container, whisk collectively the lemon juice, olive oil, thyme, rosemary, oregano, salt, and pepper.

3. Put the chicken breasts in your baking dish and pour the lemon herb marinade across them, making sure they are coated uniformly.

4. Bake in your warmed up oven for twenty-five mins or till the chicken is thoroughly cooked and make sure that it is not pink in the middle.

5. Serve using a side of steamed vegetables or a green salad.

Per serving: Calories: 250 kcal; Fat: 8gm; Carbs: 1gm; Protein: 40gm

Garlic and Herb Grilled Shrimp

Preparation time: fifteen mins

Cooking time: five mins

Servings: four

Ingredients:

• one lb. large shrimp, skinned and deveined

• three pieces garlic, crushed

• two tbsps olive oil

• one tsp dried basil

• one tsp dried parsley

• half tsp paprika

• Salt and pepper as required

Directions:

1. Warm up the grill to medium-high temp.

2. Inside your container, blend the crushed garlic, olive oil, dried basil, dried parsley, salt, paprika, and pepper.

3. Bring the shrimp to the container and toss to cover them with the garlic and herb solution.

4. Thread the shrimp onto skewers.

5. Grill the shrimp for around two-three mins on all sides till they are pink and opaque.

6. Serve with a side of quinoa or brown rice and steamed vegetables.

Per serving: Calories: 160 kcal; Fat: 7gm; Carbs: 2gm; Protein: 22gm

Veggie Stir-Fry with Tofu

Preparation time: fifteen mins

Cooking time: ten mins

Servings: four

Ingredients:

• one block firm tofu, drained and cubed

• two teacups mixed vegetables (broccoli, bell peppers, carrots, snap peas, etc.)

• two tbsps low-sodium soy sauce

• one tbsp sesame oil

• one tbsp rice vinegar

• one tsp grated ginger

• two pieces garlic, crushed

• two green onions, severed

• one tbsp sesame seeds (optional)

• Cooked quinoa or brown rice for serving

Directions:

1. Inside a big griddle or wok, warm the sesame oil at medium-high temp.

2. Include the cubed tofu and stir-fry for three-four mins till mildly browned.

3. Include the mixed vegetables then continue to stir-fry for an extra three-four mins till the vegetables are soft-crisp.

4. Inside a small container, mix the low-sodium soy sauce, rice vinegar, grated ginger, and crushed garlic.

5. Transfer the sauce across the tofu and vegetables, then toss to blend.

6. Stir in the severed green onions & sesame seeds (if using).

7. Serve the veggie stir-fry over cooked quinoa or brown rice.

Per serving: Calories: 220 kcal; Fat: 10gm; Carbs: 18gm; Protein: 15gm

Baked Cod with Mango Salsa

Preparation time: fifteen mins

Cooking time: fifteen mins

Servings: four

Ingredients:

• four cod fillets

• one ripe mango, cubed

• half red bell pepper, cubed

• quarter red onion, finely severed

• one small cucumber, cubed

• Juice of one lime

• one tbsp severed fresh cilantro

• Salt and pepper as required

Directions:

1. Warm up the oven to 375 deg.F.

2. Bring the cod fillets onto a baking tray covered using parchment paper.

3. Flavor the cod with salt and pepper.

4. Bake in your warmed up oven for twelve-fifteen mins or 'til the fish flakes simply with a fork.

5. Inside your container, blend the cubed mango, red bell pepper, red onion, cucumber, lime juice, and severed cilantro to create the mango salsa.

6. Top the baked cod with the mango salsa and serve.

Per serving: Calories: 180 kcal; Fat: 2gm; Carbs: 15gm; Protein: 25gm

Quinoa Stuffed Bell Peppers

Preparation time: twenty mins

Cooking time: twenty-five mins

Servings: four

Ingredients:

• four bell peppers (any color)

• one teacup cooked quinoa

• one teacup black beans (cooked or canned, that is drained and washed)

• one teacup cubed tomatoes (canned or fresh)

• one teacup severed spinach or kale

• one tsp cumin

• one tsp chili powder

• Salt and pepper as required

• half teacup low-sodium vegetable broth

• quarter teacup shredded low-fat cheese (optional)

Directions:

1. Warm up the oven to 375 deg.F.

2. Cut the tops off the bell peppers then take out the seeds and membranes.

3. Inside your container, blend collectively the cooked quinoa, black beans, cubed tomatoes, severed spinach or kale, cumin, chili powder, salt, and pepper.

4. Stuff each bell pepper using the quinoa mixtures and put them in a baking dish.

5. Transfer the vegetable broth into the bottom of the baking dish.

6. Conceal the dish using aluminum foil then bake for twenty mins.

7. Take out the foil, spray shredded low-fat cheese on top (if using), and bake for an extra five mins till the cheese is melted.

8. Serve the quinoa stuffed bell peppers as a tasty and nutritious meal.

Per serving: Calories: 250 kcal; Fat: 3gm; Carbs: 45gm; Protein: 12gm

Turkey and Vegetable Skillet

Preparation time: fifteen mins

Cooking time: twenty mins

Servings: four

Ingredients:

• one tbsp olive oil

• one lb. ground turkey

• one onion, severed

• two pieces garlic, crushed

• one zucchini, cubed

• one red bell pepper, cubed

• one teacup sliced mushrooms

• one tin (fourteen oz) cubed tomatoes (low-sodium)

• one tsp dried oregano

• one tsp dried basil

• Salt and pepper as required

• Fresh parsley, severed (for garnish)

Directions:

1. Inside your big griddle, warm the olive oil at middling temp.

2. Include the ground turkey then cook till browned, breaking it apart using a spoon as it cooks.

3. Include the severed onion and crushed garlic to the griddle and cook for two-three mins till they soften.

4. Stir in the cubed zucchini, red bell pepper, and sliced mushrooms, and cook for another five mins till the vegetables are soft.

5. Include the cubed tomatoes, dried oregano, dried basil, salt, and pepper to the griddle. Mix thoroughly.

6. Simmer the solution for around five mins till the flavors meld together.

7. Garnish with severed fresh parsley prior to serving.

Per serving: Calories: 280 kcal; Fat: 12gm; Carbs: 14gm; Protein: 28gm

Baked Eggplant Parmesan

Preparation time: twenty mins

Cooking time: twenty-five mins

Servings: four

Ingredients:

- one big eggplant, sliced into rounds
- one teacup whole wheat breadcrumbs
- half teacup grated Parmesan cheese
- two big eggs, beaten
- two teacups marinara sauce (low-sodium)
- one teacup shredded part-skim mozzarella cheese
- Fresh basil leaves (for garnish)

Directions:

1. Warm up the oven to 375 deg.F.

2. Dip each eggplant slice into your beaten eggs and then coat it with the whole wheat breadcrumbs mixed with grated Parmesan cheese.

3. Put the coated eggplant slices on your baking tray covered with parchment paper.

4. Bake the eggplant slices in your warmed up oven for around fifteen-twenty mins till they are soft and crispy.

5. In your baking dish, pour a fine layer of your marinara sauce.

6. Arrange the baked eggplant slices on top of the sauce.

7. Transfer the rest of the marinara sauce across the eggplant then spray shredded mozzarella cheese on top.

8. Bake for an extra ten mins or till the cheese is dissolved and bubbly.

9. Garnish with fresh basil leaves prior to serving.

Per serving: Calories: 250 kcal; Fat: 10gm; Carbs: 25gm; Protein: 15gm

Lentil and Vegetable Curry

Preparation time: fifteen mins

Cooking time: twenty-five mins

Servings: four

Ingredients:

- one teacup dried red lentils
- two teacups vegetable broth (low-sodium)
- one tbsp olive oil
- one onion, severed
- two pieces garlic, crushed
- one tbsp grated fresh ginger
- one tbsp curry powder
- one tsp ground cumin
- one tsp ground coriander
- one tin (fourteen oz) cubed tomatoes (low-sodium)
- one teacup severed spinach
- Salt and pepper as required
- Cooked brown rice (for serving)

Directions:

1. Rinse the red lentils under cold water and drain them.

2. Inside your saucepot, raise the vegetable broth to a boil and include the lentils. Cook for around ten-fifteen mins or till the lentils are soft then the liquid is immersed.

3. Inside your distinct big griddle, warm the olive oil at middling temp.

4. Include the severed onion, crushed garlic, and grated ginger to the griddle and cook for two-three mins till fragrant.

5. Stir in the curry powder, ground cumin, and ground coriander, and cook for an extra min.

6. Include the cubed tomatoes to the griddle then simmer for five mins.

7. Stir in the cooked lentils and severed spinach, and cook till the spinach wilts.

8. Flavor with salt and pepper as required.

9. Serve the lentil and vegetable curry over cooked brown rice.

Per serving: Calories: 270 kcal; Fat: 4gm; Carbs: 45gm; Protein: 15gm

Seared Tuna with Sesame Seeds

Preparation time: ten mins

Cooking time: five mins

Servings: four

Ingredients:

- four tuna steaks
- two tbsps sesame seeds
- one tbsp low-sodium soy sauce
- one tbsp rice vinegar
- one tbsp honey
- one tsp grated fresh ginger
- one tsp sesame oil
- two green onions, severed (for garnish)

Directions:

1. Pat dry the tuna steaks using a paper towel.

2. Flavor the tuna using salt and pepper, then press sesame seeds onto both sides of each tuna steak.

3. Inside a small container, blend collectively the low-sodium soy sauce, rice vinegar, honey, grated ginger, and sesame oil to create the marinade.

4. Warm a non-stick griddle at medium-high temp.

5. Sear the tuna steaks for around one-two mins on all sides till they are browned on the outside but still pink in the center.

6. Transfer the marinade into the griddle and cook for another minute, glazing the tuna with the sauce.

7. Garnish with severed green onions prior to serving.

Per serving: Calories: 200 kcal; Fat: 6gm; Carbs: 7gm; Protein: 30gm

Spaghetti Squash with Marinara Sauce

Preparation time: fifteen mins

Cooking time: forty-five mins

Servings: four

Ingredients:

- one medium spaghetti squash
- two teacups marinara sauce (low-sodium)
- Fresh basil leaves (for garnish)
- Grated Parmesan cheese (optional, for garnish)

Directions:

1. Warm up the oven to 400 deg.F.

2. Cut your spaghetti squash in half lengthwise then scoop out the seeds.

3. Bring the squash halves, cut side down, on your baking tray covered with parchment paper.

4. Bake in your warmed up oven for thirty-five to forty-five mins or 'til the squash is soft and can be simply shredded with a fork.

5. Use your fork to scrape the spaghetti squash flesh into strings, resembling spaghetti.

6. Heat the marinara sauce in your saucepan over low heat till warmed.

7. Serve the spaghetti squash topped with marinara sauce and garnished with fresh basil leaves and grated Parmesan cheese (if anticipated).

Per serving: Calories: 120 kcal; Fat: 2gm; Carbs: 20gm; Protein: 4gm

Lemon Garlic Grilled Pork Chops

Preparation time: ten mins

Cooking time: ten mins

Servings: four

Ingredients:

- four boneless pork chops
- Juice of one lemon
- two tbsps olive oil
- three pieces garlic, crushed
- one tsp dried thyme
- Salt and pepper as required

Directions:

1. Inside your container, whisk collectively the lemon juice, olive oil, crushed garlic, dried thyme, salt, and pepper.

2. Put the pork chops in your shallow dish and pour the lemon garlic marinade across them, making sure they are covered uniformly.

3. Conceal the dish and allow the pork chops marinate in the fridge for almost thirty mins (or longer if possible).

4. Warm up the grill to medium-high temp.

5. Grill your pork chops for around four to five mins on all sides, or 'til they reach an internal temperature of 145 deg.F.

6. Let the grilled pork chops rest for a couple of mins prior to serving.

Per serving: Calories: 250 kcal; Fat: 12gm; Carbs: 2gm; Protein: 30gm

Baked Stuffed Portobello Mushrooms

Preparation time: twenty mins

Cooking time: twenty-five mins

Servings: four

Ingredients:

- four big Portobello mushrooms, stems removed
- one teacup cooked quinoa
- one teacup severed spinach
- half teacup cubed tomatoes
- quarter teacup severed red onion
- two pieces garlic, crushed
- quarter teacup grated Parmesan cheese
- one tbsp balsamic vinegar
- two tbsps olive oil
- Salt and pepper as required

Directions:

1. Warm up the oven to 375 deg.F.

2. Inside a container, blend collectively cooked quinoa, severed spinach, cubed tomatoes, severed red onion, crushed garlic, grated Parmesan cheese, balsamic vinegar, olive oil, salt, and pepper.

3. Brush the outer surface of each Portobello mushroom with olive oil then put them on your baking tray.

4. Fill each mushroom cap with the quinoa solution.

5. Bake in your warmed up oven for twenty to twenty-five mins or till the mushrooms are soft and the stuffing is thoroughly warmed up.

6. Serve as a delightful and healthy appetizer or a light main course.

Per serving: Calories: 180 kcal; Fat: 9gm; Carbs: 20gm; Protein: 8gm

Teriyaki Salmon with Stir-Fried Veggies

Preparation time: fifteen mins

Cooking time: fifteen mins

Servings: four

Ingredients:

• four salmon fillets

• quarter teacup low-sodium teriyaki sauce

• two tbsps low-sodium soy sauce

• one tbsp honey

• one tbsp rice vinegar

• two tbsps olive oil, divided

• two teacups mixed vegetables (broccoli, bell peppers, carrots, snow peas, etc.)

• two pieces garlic, crushed

• one tsp grated fresh ginger

• Sesame seeds & sliced green onions (for garnish)

• Cooked brown rice (optional, for serving)

Directions:

1. Inside your container, blend collectively the teriyaki sauce, low-sodium soy sauce, honey, rice vinegar, and one tbsp of olive oil.

2. Bring the salmon fillets in a shallow dish and pour the teriyaki marinade across them. Let them marinate for around fifteen mins.

3. Inside a big griddle or wok, warm the extra one tbsp of olive oil inside a medium-high temp.

4. Include the mixed vegetables, crushed garlic, and grated ginger to the griddle and stir-fry for around five mins till the vegetables are soft-crisp.

5. Take out the vegetables from the griddle then put them away.

6. Inside the similar griddle, cook the marinated salmon fillets for around four to five mins on all sides, or till they are thoroughly cooked and flake simply with a fork.

7. Serve the teriyaki salmon over stir-fried vegetables and garnish using sesame seeds and sliced green onions.

8. Optional: Serve with cooked brown rice on the side.

Per serving: Calories: 300 kcal; Fat: 14gm; Carbs: 20gm; Protein: 25gm

Vegetarian Lettuce Wraps with Tofu

Preparation time: fifteen mins

Cooking time: fifteen mins

Servings: four

Ingredients:

• one block firm tofu, drained and crumbled

• two tbsps hoisin sauce

• one tbsp low-sodium soy sauce

• one tbsp rice vinegar

• one tsp sesame oil

• one tbsp olive oil

• one onion, severed

• two pieces garlic, crushed

• half teacup shredded carrots

• half teacup severed water chestnuts

• quarter teacup severed green onions

• Lettuce leaves (such as Boston or Bibb lettuce) for wrapping

Directions:

1. Inside a container, blend collectively hoisin sauce, low-sodium soy sauce, rice vinegar, and sesame oil.

2. Warm olive oil in a huge griddle at middling temp.

3. Put severed onion and crushed garlic to the griddle and cook till they become luminous.

4. Include crumbled tofu to the griddle then cook for a couple of mins till it begins to brown mildly.

5. Transfer the sauce solution across the tofu and stir to coat uniformly.

6. Include shredded carrots, severed water chestnuts, and severed green onions to the griddle. Stir-fry for an extra two-three mins till the vegetables are thoroughly warmed up.

7. Serve the tofu solution in lettuce leaves and wrap them like tacos.

Per serving: Calories: 180 kcal; Fat: 9gm; Carbs: 15g; Protein: 10g

Grilled Turkey Burger with Avocado

Preparation time: fifteen mins

Cooking time: fifteen mins

Servings: four

Ingredients:

- one lb. ground turkey
- quarter teacup breadcrumbs
- one egg, beaten
- two pieces garlic, crushed
- one tsp dried oregano
- one tsp dried basil
- Salt and pepper as required
- one avocado, sliced
- Lettuce leaves, tomato slices, and onion slices for garnish
- Whole-grain burger buns (optional, for serving)

Directions:

1. Inside a container, blend ground turkey, breadcrumbs, beaten egg, crushed garlic, dried oregano, dried basil, salt, and pepper. Mix thoroughly to incorporate the entire components.

2. Split your turkey solution into four similar portions and shape them into burger patties.

3. Warm up the grill to medium-high heat.

4. Grill the turkey burgers for around six-seven mins on all sides or till they are thoroughly cooked then reach an internal temp. of 165 deg.F.

5. Optional: Toast the whole-grain burger buns on the grill for a minute or two.

6. Assemble the turkey burgers by placing a cooked patty on each bun (if using), then top with sliced avocado, lettuce leaves, tomato slices, and onion slices.

7. Serve with a side of mixed greens or sweet potato fries.

Per serving: Calories: 250 kcal; Fat: 12gm; Carbs: 15gm; Protein: 20gm

Ratatouille with Brown Rice

Preparation time: twenty mins

Cooking time: thirty mins

Servings: four

Ingredients:

- one eggplant, cubed
- one zucchini, cubed
- one yellow bell pepper, cubed
- one red bell pepper, cubed
- one onion, severed
- two pieces garlic, crushed
- one tin (fourteen oz) cubed tomatoes (low-sodium)
- two tbsps tomato paste
- one tsp dried thyme
- one tsp dried basil
- one tsp dried oregano
- Salt and pepper as required
- Cooked brown rice (for serving)

Directions:

1. Inside your big griddle, warm olive oil at middling temp.

2. Include severed onion & crushed garlic to the griddle and cook till they become luminous.

3. Stir in cubed eggplant, cubed zucchini, cubed yellow and red bell peppers, then cook for around five mins till the vegetables soften.

4. Include cubed tomatoes, tomato paste, dried thyme, salt, dried basil, dried oregano, and pepper to the griddle. Mix thoroughly.

5. Lower the heat, across the griddle, then let the ratatouille simmer for around fifteen-twenty mins till the entire flavors blend together.

6. Serve the ratatouille over cooked brown rice.

Per serving: Calories: 180 kcal; Fat: 5gm; Carbs: 30gm; Protein: 5gm

Baked Stuffed Zucchini Boats

Preparation time: twenty mins

Cooking time: thirty mins

Servings: four

Ingredients:

• two big zucchinis

• one teacup cooked quinoa

• one teacup cubed tomatoes

• half teacup severed bell peppers

• quarter teacup severed red onion

• two pieces garlic, crushed

• quarter teacup grated Parmesan cheese

• one tbsp olive oil

• one tsp dried oregano

• Salt and pepper as required

Directions:

1. Warm up the oven to 375 deg. F.

2. Cut your zucchini in half lengthwise then scoop out the seeds to create "boats."

3. Inside a container, blend collectively cooked quinoa, cubed tomatoes, severed bell peppers,

severed red onion, crushed garlic, grated Parmesan cheese, olive oil, dried oregano, salt, and pepper.

4. Fill each zucchini boat with the quinoa solution.

5. Put the stuffed zucchini boats on your baking tray covered with parchment paper.

6. Bake in your warmed up oven for twenty-five to thirty mins or till the zucchinis are soft and the stuffing is thoroughly warmed up.

7. Serve the baked stuffed zucchini boats as a nutritious and satisfying dish.

Per serving: Calories: 150 kcal; Fat: 5gm; Carbs: 20gm; Protein: 8gm

Lemon Herb Baked Tilapia

Preparation time: ten mins

Cooking time: fifteen mins

Servings: four

Ingredients:

• four tilapia fillets

• Juice of one lemon

• two tbsps olive oil

• one tsp dried thyme

• one tsp dried rosemary

• one tsp dried parsley

• Salt and pepper as required

Directions:

1. Warm up the oven to 375 deg.F.

2. Inside your container, whisk collectively the lemon juice, olive oil, dried thyme, dried rosemary, dried parsley, salt, and pepper.

3. Put the tilapia fillets in your baking dish and pour the lemon herb marinade across them, ensuring they are coated uniformly.

4. Bake in your warmed up oven for twelve-fifteen mins or 'til the tilapia is thoroughly cooked and flakes simply with a fork.

5. Serve with a side of steamed vegetables or a fresh green salad.

Per serving: Calories: 150 kcal; Fat: 6gm; Carbs: 1gm; Protein: 20gm

Quinoa and Black Bean Stuffed Peppers

Preparation time: fifteen mins

Cooking time: thirty mins

Servings: four

Ingredients:

- four bell peppers (any color)
- one teacup cooked quinoa
- one tin (fourteen oz) black beans, that is drained and washed
- one teacup cubed tomatoes (canned or fresh)
- half teacup cubed red onion
- half teacup cubed bell peppers
- two pieces garlic, crushed
- one tsp ground cumin
- one tsp chili powder
- Salt and pepper as required
- quarter teacup shredded low-fat cheese (optional)

Directions:

1. Warm up the oven to 375 deg.F.

2. Cut the tops off the bell peppers then take out the seeds and membranes.

3. Inside your container, blend collectively the cooked quinoa, black beans, cubed tomatoes, cubed red onion, cubed bell peppers, crushed garlic, ground cumin, chili powder, salt, and pepper.

4. Stuff each bell pepper with the quinoa and black bean solution then place them in a baking dish.

5. Optional: Sprinkle shredded low-fat cheese on top of the stuffed peppers.

6. Conceal the dish using aluminum foil and bake for twenty mins.

7. Take the foil then bake for an extra ten mins till the peppers are soft and the filling is heated through.

8. Serve the quinoa and black bean stuffed peppers as a satisfying and nutrient-packed meal.

Per serving: Calories: 250 kcal; Fat: 4g; Carbs: 45g; Protein: 12g

Baked Chicken Drumsticks with Herbs

Preparation time: ten mins

Cooking time: forty mins

Servings: four

Ingredients:

- eight chicken drumsticks, skin removed
- two tbsps olive oil
- two pieces garlic, crushed
- one tsp dried thyme
- one tsp dried rosemary
- one tsp dried oregano
- Salt and pepper as required

Directions:

1. Warm up the oven to 400 deg.F.

2. Inside your container, blend collectively the olive oil, crushed garlic, dried thyme, dried rosemary, dried oregano, salt, and pepper.

3. Put the chicken drumsticks in a large resealable plastic bag and pour the herb marinade across them. Seal the bag then massage your marinade into the chicken to cover them uniformly.

4. Let the chicken marinate in your fridge for almost thirty mins (or longer if likely).

5. Line a baking tray using aluminum foil and place a wire rack on top. Arrange the marinated chicken drumsticks on the wire rack.

6. Bake in your warmed up oven for around thirty-five to forty mins or till the chicken is thoroughly cooked and the skin is crispy.

7. Serve the baked chicken drumsticks.

Per serving: Calories: 250 kcal; Fat: 12gm; Carbs: 1gm; Protein: 32gm

Chapter 10.   Snacks Recipes

Guacamole with Veggie Sticks

Preparation time: fifteen mins

Cooking time: zero mins

Servings: four

Ingredients:

• two ripe avocados, skinned and pitted

• one small red onion, finely severed

• one-two small tomatoes, cubed

• one jalapeno pepper, seeded & finely severed (optional, regulate to your spice preference)

• one lime, juiced

• quarter teacup severed cilantro

• Salt and pepper as required

• Assorted veggie sticks (carrot sticks, cucumber sticks, bell pepper sticks, etc.) for dipping

Directions:

1. In your medium-sized container, mash the avocados with a fork till you achieve your desired guacamole consistency (chunky or uniform).

2. Include the severed red onion, cubed tomatoes, jalapeno pepper (if using), lime juice, and severed cilantro to the container. Mix everything together till thoroughly blended.

3. Flavor the guacamole using salt and pepper as required.

4. Serve the guacamole with assorted veggie sticks for dipping.

Per serving: Calories: 180 kcal; Fat: 15gm; Carbs: 12gm; Protein: 2gm

Greek Yogurt with Mixed Berries

Preparation time: five mins

Cooking time: zero mins

Servings: two

Ingredients:

• one teacup Greek yogurt (plain, low-fat)

• one teacup mixed berries (strawberries, blueberries, raspberries)

Directions:

1. Inside a container, scoop the Greek yogurt.

2. Top the yogurt with the mixed berries.

3. You can spray a little bit honey or maple syrup on top for added sweetness if anticipated.

Per serving: Calories: 150 kcal; Fat: 3gm; Carbs: 20gm; Protein: 12gm

Rice Cakes with Hummus and Cucumber

Preparation time: five mins

Cooking time: zero mins

Servings: two

Ingredients:

• four rice cakes (choose low-sodium, whole grain rice cakes)

• half teacup hummus (store-bought or homemade, low-fat)

• one small cucumber, finely cut

Directions:

1. Disperse a generous layer of your hummus on each rice cake.

2. Top the hummus with finely cut cucumber.

3. Serve instantly.

Per serving: Calories: 180 kcal; Fat: 5gm; Carbs: 28gm; Protein: 6gm

Baked Apple Chips

Preparation time: ten mins

Cooking time: two hrs

Servings: two

Ingredients:

• two apples (use sweet varieties like Honeycrisp or Fuji)

• Cinnamon (optional)

Directions:

1. Warm up your oven to 200 deg.F.

2. Wash and thinly slice the apples into uniform rounds, about 1/8-inch dense. You can leave the skin on for added fiber and nutrients.

3. Arrange your apple slices in a single layer on your baking tray covered using parchment paper or a silicone baking mat.

4. Optionally, you can spray a little cinnamon across the apple slices for added flavor.

5. Bake the apple slices in the warmed up oven for around two hrs or till they become crispy and mildly golden.

6. Once finished, take out from the oven and allow them to cool prior to serving.

Per serving: Calories: 80 kcal; Fat: 0g; Carbs: 22g; Protein: 0g

Trail Mix with Nuts and Dried Fruits

Preparation time: five mins

Cooking time: zero mins

Servings: four

Ingredients:

• half teacup raw almonds

• half teacup raw walnuts

• quarter teacup pumpkin seeds

• quarter teacup dried cranberries (unsweetened)

• quarter teacup dried apricots, severed

• quarter teacup dried figs, severed

Directions:

1. In your mixing container, blend all your components: raw almonds, walnuts, pumpkin seeds, dried cranberries, severed dried apricots, and severed dried figs.

2. Toss everything together till well mixed.

3. Split the trail mix into individual serving portions or store it in an airtight container for later snacking.

Per serving: Calories: 200 kcal; Fat: 15gm; Carbs: 12gm; Protein: 6gm

Baked Sweet Potato Fries

Preparation time: fifteen mins

Cooking time: twenty-five mins

Servings: four

Ingredients:

• two big sweet potatoes, skinned then cut into fries-like strips

• one tbsp olive oil

• one tsp paprika

• half tsp garlic powder

• half tsp onion powder

• Salt and pepper as required

Directions:

1. Warm up your oven to 425 deg. F then line a baking tray using your parchment paper.

2. Inside a big container, toss the sweet potato strips with olive oil, paprika, garlic powder, onion powder, salt, and pepper 'til they are uniformly coated.

3. Disperse your sweet potato strips in a single layer on the prepared baking tray.

4. Bake in your warmed up oven for twenty to twenty-five mins or 'til the fries are crispy & mildly

browned, turning them midway across the cooking time for even browning.

5. Once done, take out from the oven and allow them to cool mildly prior to serving.

Per serving: Calories: 150 kcal; Fat: 4gm; Carbs: 27gm; Protein: 2gm

Veggie Sushi Rolls with Avocado

Preparation time: twenty mins

Cooking time: zero mins

Servings: four

Ingredients:

• four nori seaweed sheets

• two teacups cooked sushi rice (prepared using the package instructions)

• one ripe avocado, sliced

• half cucumber, julienned

• half red bell pepper, julienned

• one carrot, julienned

• Pickled ginger and low-sodium soy sauce for serving (optional)

Directions:

1. Lay a bamboo sushi rolling mat on a clean surface. Put a nori sheet shiny side down on the mat.

2. Moisten your hands to prevent sticking, then disperse a thin, even layer of sushi rice across the nori sheet, leaving about one inch of nori at the top edge.

3. Arrange the sliced avocado, julienned cucumber, red bell pepper, and carrot along the center of the rice.

4. Carefully lift the edge of your bamboo mat closest to you and start rolling the nori sheet across the fillings, using the mat to shape the roll.

5. Moisten the top edge of your nori sheet using water to seal the roll.

6. Continue rolling till you reach the exposed edge of the nori. Apply gentle pressure to seal the roll.

7. Repeat the process using the rest of the nori sheets and stuffings.

8. Slice each sushi roll into bite-sized pieces using a sharp knife.

9. Serve with pickled ginger and low-sodium soy sauce for dipping, if anticipated.

Per serving: Calories: 200 kcal; Fat: 7gm; Carbs: 30gm; Protein: 4gm

Cottage Cheese with Pineapple Chunks

Preparation time: five mins

Cooking time: zero mins

Servings: two

Ingredients:

• one teacup low-fat cottage cheese

• one teacup fresh pineapple chunks

Directions:

1. Inside a container, scoop the low-fat cottage cheese.

2. Include the fresh pineapple chunks on top.

3. You can spray a little cinnamon or spray honey across the cottage cheese and pineapple for added flavor if anticipated.

Per serving: Calories: 150 kcal; Fat: 2gm; Carbs: 20gm; Protein: 14gm

Almond Butter and Banana Rice Cakes

Preparation time: five mins

Cooking time: zero mins

Servings: two

Ingredients:

• four rice cakes (choose low-sodium, whole grain rice cakes)

• four tbsps almond butter (unsweetened)

Directions:

1. Disperse one tbsp of your almond butter on every rice cake.

2. Top each rice cake with banana slices.

3. Serve instantly.

Per serving: Calories: 200 kcal; Fat: 9gm; Carbs: 28gm; Protein: 6gm

Baked Kale Chips

Preparation time: ten mins

Cooking time: fifteen mins

Servings: two

Ingredients:

• one bunch of kale, washed, dried, & torn into bite-sized pieces (take out tough stems)

• one tbsp olive oil

• Salt and pepper as required

Directions:

1. Warm up your oven to 350 deg.F.

2. Inside a big container, toss the kale pieces with olive oil, salt, and pepper 'til uniformly covered.

3. Disperse your kale pieces in a single layer on your baking tray covered using parchment paper.

4. Bake in your warmed up oven for ten to fifteen mins or 'til the kale is crispy and mildly golden.

5. Once done, take out from the oven and allow them to cool mildly prior to serving.

Per serving: Calories: 80 kcal; Fat: 4gm; Carbs: 10gm; Protein: 4gm

Roasted Chickpeas with Spices

Preparation time: ten mins

Cooking time: thirty mins

Servings: four

Ingredients:

• two teacups cooked chickpeas (canned or soaked and cooked)

• one tbsp olive oil

• one tsp ground cumin

• half tsp smoked paprika

• half tsp garlic powder

• Salt and pepper as required

Directions:

1. Warm up your oven to 400 deg.F.

2. Inside a container, toss the cooked chickpeas with olive oil, ground cumin, smoked paprika, garlic powder, salt, and pepper till thoroughly covered.

3. Disperse your chickpeas in a single layer onto a baking tray covered with parchment paper.

4. Bake in your warmed up oven for twenty-five to thirty mins or till the chickpeas are crispy and golden.

5. Once done, take out from the oven and allow them to cool mildly prior to serving.

Per serving: Calories: 150 kcal; Fat: 5gm; Carbs: 20gm; Protein: 6gm

Fresh Fruit Skewers with Greek Yogurt Dip

Preparation time: fifteen mins

Cooking time: zero mins

Servings: four

Ingredients:

• Assorted fresh fruits (e.g., strawberries, grapes, melon, pineapple, kiwi)

• one teacup Greek yogurt (plain, low-fat)

• one tbsp honey (optional)

Directions:

1. Wash and prepare the fresh fruits by cutting them into bite-sized pieces or leaving them as whole berries (if using grapes).

2. Thread the fruit pieces onto wooden skewers or toothpicks, creating colorful fruit skewers.

3. Inside your small container, mix the Greek yogurt with honey (if using) to create a mildly sweetened dip.

4. Serve the fruit skewers with the Greek yogurt dip on the side.

Per serving: Calories: 120 kcal; Fat: 1gm; Carbs: 25gm; Protein: 5gm

Zucchini and Carrot Fritters

Preparation time: twenty mins

Cooking time: fifteen mins

Servings: four

Ingredients:

• one medium zucchini, grated

• one medium carrot, grated

• quarter teacup whole wheat flour or your chickpea flour

• two green onions, finely severed

• two tbsps severed fresh parsley

• one tsp ground cumin

• Salt and pepper as required

• one-two tbsps olive oil for frying

Directions:

1. Inside a big container, blend the grated zucchini, grated carrot, whole wheat flour or chickpea flour, severed green onions, severed parsley, ground cumin, salt, and pepper. Mix till thoroughly blended.

2. Warm olive oil in your non-stick griddle at middling temp.

3. Take a spoonful of the fritter solution and flatten it in your hands to form a small patty. Repeat with the rest of the solution.

4. Fry the fritters in the hot griddle for around three-four mins on all sides or till they are golden brown and crispy.

5. Once done, transfer the fritters to a plate covered using paper towels to absorb any extra oil.

6. Serve the zucchini and carrot fritters warm.

Per serving: Calories: 90 kcal; Fat: 4gm; Carbs: 10gm; Protein: 3gm

Beet Chips with Sea Salt

Preparation time: ten mins

Cooking time: twenty mins

Servings: two

Ingredients:

• two medium beets, skinned and finely cut

• one tbsp olive oil

• Sea salt as required

Directions:

1. Warm up your oven to 375 deg.F.

2. Inside your container, toss the beet slices with olive oil till they are uniformly coated.

3. Arrange your beet slices in a single layer on your baking tray covered using parchment paper.

4. Sprinkle sea salt across the beet slices.

5. Bake in to your warmed up oven for twenty mins or till the beet chips are crispy and mildly curled at the edges.

6. Once done, take out from the oven and allow them to cool mildly prior to serving.

Per serving: Calories: 80 kcal; Fat: 4gm; Carbs: 10gm; Protein: 2gm

Caprese Skewers with Cherry Tomatoes and Mozzarella

Preparation time: ten mins **Cooking time:** zero mins

Servings: four

Ingredients:

- Cherry tomatoes
- Fresh mozzarella balls (bocconcini)
- Fresh basil leaves
- Balsamic glaze (optional, for drizzling)

Directions:

1. Wash the cherry tomatoes and fresh basil leaves.

2. Thread a cherry tomato, a mozzarella ball, and a fresh basil leaf onto small wooden skewers or toothpicks.

3. Repeat with the remaining components to create caprese skewers.

4. If anticipated, spray a little bit of balsamic glaze across the caprese skewers prior to serving.

Per serving: Calories: 100 kcal; Fat: 7gm; Carbs: 2gm; Protein: 6gm

Chapter 11. Special Vegetable Recipes

Stuffed Bell Peppers with Quinoa and Beans

Preparation time: twenty mins

Cooking time: thirty mins

Servings: four

Ingredients:

- four big bell peppers (any color)
- one teacup cooked quinoa
- one teacup cooked black beans
- one teacup cubed tomatoes
- one teacup cubed zucchini
- half teacup cubed onion
- two pieces garlic, crushed
- one tsp cumin
- one tsp chili powder
- Salt and pepper as required
- Olive oil (for brushing)

Directions:

1. Warm up the oven to 375 deg.F.

2. Cut the tops off your bell peppers then take out the seeds and membranes.

3. Inside a big blending container, blend cooked quinoa, black beans, cubed tomatoes, cubed zucchini, onion, garlic, cumin, chili powder, salt, and pepper.

4. Stuff each bell pepper with the quinoa and bean solution.

5. Bring the stuffed peppers in a baking dish, brush them mildly with olive oil, and cover with aluminum foil.

6. Bake in your warmed up oven for twenty-five to thirty mins till the peppers are soft.

Per serving: Calories: 240 kcal; Fat: 3gm; Carbs: 45gm; Protein: 11gm

Cauliflower Rice Stir-Fry with Tofu

Preparation time: fifteen mins

Cooking time: fifteen mins

Servings: two

Ingredients:

- one small head cauliflower, grated or processed into rice-like consistency
- eight oz tofu, cubed
- one teacup broccoli florets
- one teacup sliced bell peppers (any color)
- one teacup sliced carrots
- two pieces garlic, crushed
- one tbsp low-sodium soy sauce
- one tbsp sesame oil
- one tbsp rice vinegar
- one tbsp severed green onions (for garnish)

Directions:

1. Warm sesame oil in a huge griddle at middling temp.

2. Include crushed garlic and sauté for a min till fragrant.

3. Include tofu cubes and stir-fry for three-four mins till mildly browned.

4. Include sliced bell peppers, carrots, and broccoli. Stir-fry for another three-four mins till vegetables are soft-crisp.

5. Stir in the cauliflower rice then cook for an extra two-three mins.

6. Spray soy sauce and rice vinegar across the stir-fry and toss everything together till well blended.

7. Garnish with severed green onions prior to serving.

Per serving: Calories: 250 kcal; Fat: 10gm; Carbs: 25gm; Protein: 18gm

Spinach and Mushroom Stuffed Portobello Caps

Preparation time: fifteen mins

Cooking time: twenty mins

Servings: two

Ingredients:

- four big portobello mushroom caps
- two teacups fresh spinach, severed
- one teacup cubed mushrooms
- half teacup cubed onion
- two pieces garlic, crushed
- one tbsp olive oil
- quarter teacup low-fat feta cheese (optional)
- Salt and pepper as required

Directions:

1. Warm up the oven to 375 deg.F.

2. Take the stems from the portobello mushroom caps and carefully clean them using a damp cloth.

3. In your griddle, warm olive oil at middling temp. Include cubed onions and crushed garlic, sautéing till onions are luminous.

4. Include cubed mushrooms and severed spinach to the griddle. Cook till the vegetables are soft.

5. Flavor the filling using salt and pepper as required.

6. Fill each portobello mushroom cap with the spinach and mushroom solution.

7. If anticipated, spray some low-fat feta cheese on top of each stuffed mushroom cap.

8. Put the stuffed mushrooms on your baking tray and bake for around fifteen-twenty mins till the mushrooms are thoroughly cooked.

Per serving: Calories: 180 kcal; Fat: 8gm; Carbs: 15gm; Protein: 12gm

Baked Sweet Potatoes with Quinoa and Pomegranate Seeds

Preparation time: ten mins

Cooking time: forty-five mins

Servings: two

Ingredients:

- two medium sweet potatoes
- one teacup cooked quinoa
- half teacup pomegranate seeds
- quarter teacup severed fresh parsley
- one tbsp lemon juice
- Salt and pepper as required

Directions:

1. Warm up the oven to 400 deg.F.

2. Wash your sweet potatoes and prick them numerous occasions with a fork.

3. Put the sweet potatoes on your baking tray then bake for around forty to forty-five mins or till soft.

4. In a mixing container, blend cooked quinoa, salt, pomegranate seeds, severed parsley, lemon juice, and pepper.

5. Once the sweet potatoes are done baking, slice them open and stuff with the quinoa and pomegranate solution.

Per serving: Calories: 350 kcal; Fat: 4gm; Carbs: 72gm; Protein: 9gm

Lentil and Vegetable Shepherd's Pie

Preparation time: twenty mins

Cooking time: forty mins

Servings: four

Ingredients:

- one teacup cooked lentils
- one teacup mixed vegetables (carrots, peas, corn)
- half teacup cubed onions
- two pieces garlic, crushed
- one teacup vegetable broth
- one tbsp tomato paste
- one tbsp olive oil
- two teacups mashed sweet potatoes or cauliflower (for topping)
- Salt and pepper as required

Directions:

1. Warm up the oven to 375 deg.F.

2. Inside your big griddle, warm olive oil at middling temp. Include cubed onions and crushed garlic, sautéing till onions are luminous.

3. Include mixed vegetables to the griddle and cook till they are soft.

4. Stir in the cooked lentils, vegetable broth, and tomato paste. Simmer for a couple of mins till the solution denses mildly.

5. Flavor using salt and pepper as required.

6. Put the lentil and vegetable solution to a baking dish.

7. Disperse the mashed sweet potatoes or cauliflower across the top of the lentil solution.

8. Bake in your warmed up oven for twenty-five to thirty mins or till the topping is lightly browned.

Per serving: Calories: 320 kcal; Fat: 5gm; Carbs: 54gm; Protein: 14gm

Zucchini Noodles with Pesto and Cherry Tomatoes

Preparation time: fifteen mins

Cooking time: five mins

Servings: two

Ingredients:

- two medium zucchinis, spiralized or finely cut
- one teacup cherry tomatoes, halved
- two tbsps homemade or store-bought pesto sauce (without cheese)
- one tbsp pine nuts (optional)
- Fresh basil leaves for garnish
- Salt and pepper as required

Directions:

1. Inside a big griddle, sauté the zucchini noodles at middling temp. for around two-three mins till they are just soft.

2. Bring the halved cherry tomatoes to the griddle and sauté for an extra min.

3. Stir in the pesto sauce and toss everything together till well blended.

4. If using pine nuts, toast them in a separate dry griddle till lightly golden and then spray them across the zucchini noodles.

5. Flavor with salt and pepper as required.

6. Garnish with fresh basil leaves prior to serving.

Per serving: Calories: 220 kcal; Fat: 15gm; Carbs: 17gm; Protein: 8gm

Stuffed Acorn Squash with Wild Rice & Cranberries

Preparation time: fifteen mins

Cooking time: forty-five mins

Servings: two

Ingredients:

- one acorn squash, halved and seeds taken out
- one teacup cooked wild rice
- quarter teacup dried cranberries
- quarter teacup severed pecans or walnuts
- one tbsp olive oil
- one tbsp balsamic vinegar
- Salt and pepper as required

Directions:

1. Warm up the oven to 375 deg.F.

2. Put the acorn squash halves, cut side up, onto a baking tray.

3. Inside a container, mix the cooked wild rice, dried cranberries, severed nuts, olive oil, and balsamic vinegar.

4. Stuff each acorn squash half with the wild rice solution.

5. Flavor with salt and pepper as required.

6. Conceal the baking tray using aluminum foil and bake for around thirty to thirty-five mins or till the squash is soft.

Per serving: Calories: 320 kcal; Fat: 15gm; Carbs: 45gm; Protein: 5gm

Roasted Eggplant with Tahini Dressing

Preparation time: ten mins

Cooking time: twenty-five mins

Servings: two

Ingredients:

- one big eggplant, sliced into rounds or half-moons
- two tbsps olive oil
- two tbsps tahini
- two tbsps lemon juice
- one piece garlic, crushed
- two tbsps water (or more, as needed)
- Fresh parsley for garnish
- Salt and pepper as required

Directions:

1. Warm up the oven to 400 deg.F.

2. Put the eggplant slices on your baking tray and spray with olive oil. Flavor with salt and pepper.

3. Roast your eggplant in the warmed up oven for around twenty to twenty-five mins till they are soft and mildly browned.

4. Inside your small container, whisk collectively tahini, lemon juice, crushed garlic, and water to create a uniform dressing. Put extra water if required to achieve your anticipated uniformity.

5. Arrange the roasted eggplant on a serving plate and spray the tahini dressing across them.

6. Garnish with fresh parsley prior to serving.

Per serving: Calories: 220 kcal; Fat: 18gm; Carbs: 15gm; Protein: 4gm

Brussels Sprouts and Apple Hash

Preparation time: ten mins

Cooking time: fifteen mins

Servings: two

Ingredients:

- two teacups Brussels sprouts, clipped and halved
- one big apple, cubed (use a variety that's not overly sweet)
- half teacup cubed onion
- one tbsp olive oil
- one tbsp apple cider vinegar

• one tbsp maple syrup (optional, for your touch of sweetness)

• Salt and pepper as required

Directions:

1. Inside a big griddle, warm olive oil in a middling temp.

2. Include cubed onions and sauté till they become luminous.

3. Include halved Brussels sprouts to the griddle and cook for around five-seven mins till they are soft-crisp.

4. Stir in the cubed apple then cook for another two-three mins till the apple is mildly softened.

5. Include apple cider vinegar and maple syrup (if using) to the griddle. Toss everything together till thoroughly blended.

6. Flavor with salt and pepper as required.

7. Serve as a side dish or with a protein of your choice.

Per serving: Calories: 180 kcal; Fat: 7gm; Carbs: 28gm; Protein: 3gm

Cabbage and Carrot Spring Rolls with Peanut Sauce

Preparation time: thirty mins

Cooking time: ten mins

Servings: four

Ingredients:

• eight rice paper wrappers

• two teacups shredded cabbage

• one teacup shredded carrots

• one cucumber, julienned

• one avocado, sliced

• Fresh cilantro leaves

• Fresh mint leaves

• quarter teacup natural peanut butter

• one tbsp soy sauce

• one tbsp maple syrup

• one tbsp lime juice

• two tbsps warm water (or more, as needed)

Directions:

1. Prepare the entire vegetables for the spring rolls and set them aside.

2. Fill a huge shallow dish with warm water. Dip your one rice paper wrapper into the water for a few seconds 'til it becomes soft and pliable.

3. Lay the softened rice paper on your clean, damp kitchen towel or a silicone rolling mat.

4. At the center of the rice paper, place a small amount of shredded cabbage, carrots, julienned cucumber, avocado slices, cilantro, and mint leaves.

5. Wrap the ends of the rice paper over the topping, after which securely coil it up.

6. Repeat the process using the rest of the rice paper wrappers and filling components.

7. For the peanut sauce, whisk collectively peanut butter, soy sauce, maple syrup, lime juice, and warm water inside a small container till uniform and creamy. Put additional water if required to achieve your anticipated uniformity.

8. Serve the spring rolls with your peanut sauce for dipping.

Per serving: Calories: 270 kcal; Fat: 15gm; Carbs: 30gm; Protein: 8gm

Butternut Squash and Kale Salad with Maple-Dijon Dressing

Preparation time: fifteen mins

Cooking time: twenty mins

Servings: two

Ingredients:

- two teacups cubed butternut squash
- two teacups severed kale leaves
- quarter teacup dried cranberries
- quarter teacup severed walnuts
- two tbsps olive oil
- one tbsp balsamic vinegar
- one tbsp pure maple syrup
- one tsp Dijon mustard
- Salt and pepper as required

Directions:

1. Warm up the oven to 400 deg.F.

2. Put your cubed butternut squash on your baking tray and spray using one tbsp of olive oil. Flavor using salt and pepper.

3. Roast the butternut squash in your warmed up oven for around twenty mins or till soft and mildly caramelized.

4. Inside a big container, massage the severed kale leaves with your remaining one tbsp of olive oil for a couple of mins till the leaves become soft.

5. Include the roasted butternut squash, dried cranberries, and severed walnuts to the container with kale.

6. Inside your small container, whisk collectively balsamic vinegar, maple syrup, & Dijon mustard to create the dressing.

7. Transfer the dressing across the salad and toss the whole thing together till well blended.

Per serving: Calories: 320 kcal; Fat: 18gm; Carbs: 38gm; Protein: 5gm

Grilled Asparagus with Lemon-Tahini Sauce

Preparation time: ten mins

Cooking time: eight mins

Servings: two

Ingredients:

- one bunch asparagus spears, tough ends clipped
- one tbsp olive oil
- Salt and pepper as required
- two tbsps tahini
- one tbsp lemon juice
- two tbsps water (or more, as required)

Directions:

1. Warm up your grill or your grill pot at medium-high temp.

2. Spray the asparagus spears using olive oil and flavor with salt and pepper.

3. Grill the asparagus for around four mins on all sides till they are soft and lightly charred.

4. Inside your small container, whisk collectively tahini, lemon juice, and water to create a uniform sauce. Put additional water if required to achieve your anticipated uniformity.

5. Spray the lemon-tahini sauce across the grilled asparagus prior to serving.

Per serving: Calories: 160 kcal; Fat: 13gm; Carbs: 9gm; Protein: 6gm

Beet and Goat Cheese Salad with Walnuts & Balsamic Glaze

Preparation time: fifteen mins

Cooking time: one hr (for roasting beets)

Servings: two

Ingredients:

• two medium beets, roasted, skinned, and sliced

• two teacups mixed salad greens (spinach, arugula, or mixed greens)

• quarter teacup crumbled goat cheese

• quarter teacup severed walnuts

• two tbsps balsamic glaze (store-bought or homemade)

• Salt and pepper as required

Directions:

1. Warm up the oven to 400 deg.F.

2. Wrap the beets individually in your aluminum foil then roast in your warmed up oven for around one hr or till they are soft.

3. Let the roasted beets cool mildly, then peel and slice them.

4. Inside a salad container, blend the mixed salad greens with the sliced beets.

5. Sprinkle crumbled goat cheese & severed walnuts across the salad.

6. Spray balsamic glaze across the salad and flavor with salt and pepper as required.

7. Toss everything together carefully prior to serving.

Per serving: Calories: 280 kcal; Fat: 17gm; Carbs: 24gm; Protein: 8gm

Steamed Artichokes with Lemon and Garlic

Preparation time: ten mins

Cooking time: twenty-five mins

Servings: two

Ingredients:

• two big artichokes

• two pieces garlic, crushed

• two tbsps lemon juice

• one tbsp olive oil

• Salt and pepper as required

Directions:

1. Trim the stems of the artichokes then take out any tough outer leaves.

2. Cut off the top inch of each artichoke and use kitchen scissors to trim the sharp tips of the remaining leaves.

3. Put the artichokes in a steamer basket over boiling water, cover, and steam for around twenty to twenty-five mins or till the leaves pull away simply and the hearts are soft.

4. Inside your small container, mix crushed garlic, salt, lemon juice, olive oil, and pepper to create a dipping sauce.

5. Serve the steamed artichokes with the lemon and garlic sauce on the side.

Per serving: Calories: 150 kcal; Fat: 7gm; Carbs: 20gm; Protein: 5gm

Roasted Fennel with Parmesan Cheese

Preparation time: ten mins

Cooking time: twenty-five mins

Servings: two

Ingredients:

- two medium fennel bulbs, sliced
- two tbsps olive oil
- quarter teacup grated Parmesan cheese
- Salt and pepper as required

Directions:

1. Warm up the oven to 400 deg.F.

2. Toss the sliced fennel bulbs with olive oil, salt, and pepper in a mixing container.

3. Disperse the fennel slices in a single layer onto a baking tray.

4. Roast in your warmed up oven for around twenty to twenty-five mins or 'til the fennel is soft and mildly caramelized.

5. Take out the roasted fennel from your oven and spray grated Parmesan cheese across the top.

Per serving: Calories: 190 kcal; Fat: 14gm; Carbs: 13gm; Protein: 6gm

Download your Bonus now, frame the QR code

Chapter 12. Dessert Recipes

Mixed Berry Parfait with Greek Yogurt

Preparation time: ten mins

Cooking time: zero mins

Servings: two

Ingredients:

• one teacup mixed berries (strawberries, blueberries, raspberries)

• one teacup Greek yogurt (low-fat or non-fat)

• one tbsp honey (optional for sweetness)

• quarter teacup granola (choose one with low sugar content)

Directions:

1. Wash your berries then pat them dry with a paper towel.

2. Inside your container, mix the Greek yogurt with honey (if using) to include sweetness.

3. In serving glasses or containers, layer the Greek yogurt and mixed berries.

4. Top using a spray of granola for added crunch.

5. Serve instantly or refrigerate for later.

Per serving: Calories: 180 kcal; Fat: 3gm; Carbs: 30gm; Protein: 11gm

Baked Apples with Cinnamon and Honey

Preparation time: fifteen mins

Cooking time: thirty mins

Servings: four

Ingredients:

• four apples (any variety, like Granny Smith or Honeycrisp)

• one tsp ground cinnamon

• two tbsps honey

• quarter teacup water

Directions:

1. Warm up the oven to 375 deg.F.

2. Core the apples and place them in a baking dish.

3. Mix cinnamon and honey in your small container, then spray the solution across the apples.

4. Pour water into the baking dish to prevent the apples from sticking.

5. Bake in to your warmed up oven for thirty mins or 'til the apples are soft.

6. Take out from the oven and allow them to cool mildly prior to serving.

Per serving: Calories: 110 kcal; Fat: 0.3gm; Carbs: 29gm; Protein: 0.4gm

Chia Seed Pudding with Coconut Milk & Fresh Fruit

Preparation time: five mins (plus chilling time)

Cooking time: zero mins

Servings: two

Ingredients:

• quarter teacup chia seeds

• one teacup coconut milk (unsweetened)

• one tbsp honey (or more as required)

• Fresh fruit of your choice (e.g., sliced strawberries, blueberries, or mango)

Directions:

1. Inside a container, mix chia seeds, coconut milk, and honey.

2. Stir thoroughly to ensure your chia seeds are uniformly distributed.

3. Cover and put the solution in the fridge for almost two hrs or overnight to let it to thicken.

4. When ready to serve, layer the chia seed pudding with fresh fruit in small jars or glasses.

Per serving: Calories: 250 kcal; Fat: 16gm; Carbs: 21gm; Protein: 5gm

Mango and Lime Sorbet

Preparation time: ten mins (plus freezing time)

Cooking time: zero mins

Servings: four

Ingredients:

• two ripe mangoes, skinned and cubed

• Juice of one lime

• two tbsps honey (or agave syrup)

Directions:

1. Put the cubed mangoes in your mixer or blending container.

2. Include lime juice and honey (or agave syrup) to the mixer.

3. Blend till you get a uniform puree.

4. Put the solution into a shallow, freezer-safe container.

5. Freeze for almost four hrs, stirring every hour to break up any ice crystals.

6. Once frozen, scoop the sorbet into serving containers or glasses.

Per serving: Calories: 120 kcal; Fat: 0.5gm; Carbs: 31gm; Protein: 1gm

Dark Chocolate-Dipped Strawberries

Preparation time: ten mins (plus cooling time)

Cooking time: zero mins

Servings: two

Ingredients:

• one teacup strawberries, washed and patted dry

• two oz dark chocolate (70% cocoa or higher)

Directions:

1. Cover a tray with parchment paper.

2. Inside your microwave-safe container, melt the dark chocolate in your microwave, stirring every 15-20 seconds till uniform.

3. Dip each strawberry into your melted chocolate, covering about half of the fruit.

4. Put the dipped strawberries on the prepared tray.

5. Allow the chocolate to cool then set prior to serving.

Per serving: Calories: 120 kcal; Fat: 7gm; Carbs: 14gm; Protein: 2gm

Grilled Pineapple with Mint and Honey

Preparation time: ten mins

Cooking time: eight mins

Servings: four

Ingredients:

• one pineapple, skinned, cored, then sliced into rings or wedges

• two tbsps honey

• Fresh mint leaves for garnish

Directions:

1. Warm up your grill or your grill pan at middling temp.

2. Grill your pineapple slices for around three-four mins on all sides till they have grill marks.

3. Take out the grilled pineapple from the heat and spray honey across them.

4. Garnish with fresh mint leaves prior to serving.

Per serving: Calories: 80 kcal; Fat: 0.2gm; Carbs: 21gm; Protein: 0.7gm

Baked Pears with Walnuts and Honey

Preparation time: ten mins

Cooking time: twenty mins

Servings: four

Ingredients:

- four ripe pears, halved and cored
- quarter teacup severed walnuts
- two tbsps honey

Directions:

1. Warm up the oven to 375 deg.F.

2. Put the pear halves on your baking tray, cut-side up.

3. Sprinkle severed walnuts over each pear half and spray honey on top.

4. Bake in to your warmed up oven for twenty mins or till the pears are soft.

5. Take out from the oven and allow them to cool mildly prior to serving.

Per serving: Calories: 130 kcal; Fat: 5gm; Carbs: 25gm; Protein: 1.5gm

Banana Nice Cream with Almond Butter

Preparation time: five mins (plus freezing time)

Cooking time: zero mins

Servings: two

Ingredients:

- two ripe bananas, skinned and sliced
- two tbsps almond butter (unsweetened)

Directions:

1. Put the sliced bananas in a sealed container and freeze them for almost two hrs or till solid.

2. Once frozen, transfer the bananas to a mixer or blending container.

3. Include almond butter to the mixer.

4. Blend till you achieve a creamy, ice cream-like texture.

5. Serve instantly or return to the freezer for a firmer consistency.

Per serving: Calories: 200 kcal; Fat: 8gm; Carbs: 30gm; Protein: 4gm

Cinnamon Baked Peaches

Preparation time: ten mins

Cooking time: twenty-five mins

Servings: four

Ingredients:

- four ripe peaches, halved and pitted
- one tbsp honey
- half tsp ground cinnamon

Directions:

1. Warm up the oven to 375 deg.F.

2. Put the peach halves on your baking sheet, cut-side up.

3. Spray honey over each peach half and spray ground cinnamon on top.

4. Bake in to your warmed up oven for around twenty-five mins or till the peaches are soft and caramelized.

5. Take out from the oven and allow them to cool mildly prior to serving.

Per serving: Calories: 60 kcal; Fat: 0.2gm; Carbs: 16gm; Protein: 1gm

Banana Oat Cookies

Preparation time: fifteen mins

Cooking time: fifteen mins

Servings: twelve cookies

Ingredients:

- two ripe bananas, mashed
- one teacup rolled oats
- quarter teacup unsweetened applesauce
- quarter teacup severed nuts (e.g., almonds, pecans, or walnuts)
- quarter teacup dried fruits (e.g., raisins, cranberries, or severed dates)
- one tsp ground cinnamon
- half tsp vanilla extract

Directions:

1. Warm up your oven to 350 deg. F then cover baking sheet using parchment paper.

2. Inside your blending container, blend the mashed bananas, unsweetened applesauce, and vanilla extract. Mix well till you get a uniform solution.

3. Include the rolled oats, severed nuts, dried fruits, and ground cinnamon to the container with the banana solution. Stir 'til the entire components are uniformly incorporated.

4. Let the solution sit for around five mins to let the oats to absorb some of the moisture.

5. Using a spoon or your hands, scoop about 1.5 tablespoons of the cookie dough and drop it onto the prepared baking sheet. Flatten the dough slightly to form a cookie shape.

6. Repeat the process with your remaining dough, leaving some space between each cookie on the baking sheet.

7. Bake the cookies in the warmed up oven for approximately fifteen mins or till they turn golden brown around the edges.

8. Once baked, take the cookies from the oven then let them cool on the baking sheet for a couple of mins prior to moving them to your wire rack to cool completely.

9. Enjoy these naturally sweetened and fiber-rich banana oat cookies as a healthy treat for your fatty liver-friendly diet!

Per serving: Calories: 85 kcal Fat: 3gm Carbs: 14gm Fiber: 2gm Sugar: 5gm Protein: 2gm

8 - Week Meal Plan

Week 1:

Day	Breakfast	Lunch	Dinner	Dessert
1	Fruit Salad with Mint and Lime Dressing	Grilled Chicken Salad with Mixed Greens	Tuna and Avocado Salad	Baked Apples with Cinnamon and Honey
2	Veggie and Mushroom Scramble	Lemon Garlic Shrimp Scampi	Lemon Pepper Tilapia	Banana Oat Cookies
3	Greek Yogurt Parfait with Nuts and Honey	Grilled Mackerel with Lime and Cilantro	Quinoa Stuffed Bell Peppers	Baked Pears with Walnuts and Honey
4	Smoothie Bowl with Kale and Mixed Berries	Turkey and Veggie Wrap with Whole Grain Tortilla	Turkey and Vegetable Skillet	Dark Chocolate-Dipped Strawberries
5	Quinoa Breakfast Bowl with Almond Milk	Zucchini Noodles with Pesto Sauce	Baked Eggplant Parmesan	Banana Nice Cream with Almond Butter
6	Vegetable Frittata with Egg Whites	Sweet Potato and Black Bean Chili	Baked Stuffed Portobello Mushrooms	Mango and Lime Sorbet
7	Chia Seed Pudding with Fruit Compote	Baked Chicken Thighs with Rosemary and Lemon	Ratatouille with Brown Rice	Cinnamon Baked Peaches

Week 2:

Day	Breakfast	Lunch	Dinner	Dessert
1	Breakfast Burrito with Black Beans and Salsa	Lentil and Vegetable Soup	Baked Cod with Lemon and Dill	Chia Seed Pudding with Coconut Milk & Fresh Fruit
2	Brown Rice Porridge with Cinnamon and Apples	Baked Haddock with Herbed Bread Crumbs	Lentil and Vegetable Curry	Mixed Berry Parfait with Greek Yogurt
3	Blueberry Almond Overnight Oats	Baked Chicken Meatloaf with Spinach	Lemon Herb Baked Chicken Breast	Grilled Pineapple with Mint and Honey
4	Whole Grain Pancakes with Fresh Fruit Toppings	Sardine and Tomato Salad	Garlic and Herb Grilled Shrimp	Baked Apples with Cinnamon and Honey
5	Veggie Omelet with Spinach and Tomatoes	Pork Stir-Fry with Bok Choy And Garlic	Baked Salmon with Lemon and Herbs	Banana Oat Cookies
6	Avocado Toast with Poached Egg	Baked Salmon with Steamed Asparagus	Lemon Garlic Grilled Pork Chops	Baked Pears with Walnuts and Honey
7	Banana Walnut Muffins	Baked Cod with Mediterranean Salsa	Lean Beef Kebabs with Bell Peppers and Onions	Dark Chocolate-Dipped Strawberries

Week 3:

Day	Breakfast	Lunch	Dinner	Dessert
1	Oatmeal with Fresh Berries	Anchovy and Tomato Bruschetta	Baked Stuffed Zucchini Boats	Mango and Lime Sorbet
2	Fruit Salad with Mint and Lime Dressing	Lean Beef and Vegetable Stir-Fry	Teriyaki Salmon with Stir-Fried Veggies	Cinnamon Baked Peaches
3	Veggie and Mushroom Scramble	Baked Trout with Garlic and Olive Oil	Vegetarian Lettuce Wraps with Tofu	Chia Seed Pudding with Coconut Milk & Fresh Fruit
4	Greek Yogurt Parfait with Nuts and Honey	Poached Salmon with Cucumber-Dill Sauce	Grilled Turkey Burger with Avocado	Mixed Berry Parfait with Greek Yogurt
5	Smoothie Bowl with Kale and Mixed Berries	Baked Snapper with Tomatoes and Olives	Miso-Glazed Black Cod	Banana Nice Cream with Almond Butter
6	Vegetable Frittata with Egg Whites	Eggplant and Chickpea Curry	Grilled Halibut with Mango Salsa	Baked Apples with Cinnamon and Honey
7	Chia Seed Pudding with Fruit Compote	Baked Chicken Drumsticks with Herbs	Steamed Fish with Ginger and Soy Sauce	Dark Chocolate-Dipped Strawberries

Week 4:

Day	Breakfast	Lunch	Dinner	Dessert
1	Breakfast Burrito with Black Beans and Salsa	Turkey and Vegetable Stir-Fry	Grilled Skinless Chicken Breast with Herbs	Cinnamon Baked Peaches
2	Brown Rice Porridge with Cinnamon and Apples	Chickpea and Roasted Vegetable Bowl	Baked Pork Tenderloin with Apple Chutney	Mango and Lime Sorbet
3	Blueberry Almond Overnight Oats	Thai Shrimp Lettuce Wraps	Beef Stir-Fry with Broccoli and Snow Peas	Chia Seed Pudding with Coconut Milk & Fresh Fruit
4	Whole Grain Pancakes with Fresh Fruit Toppings	Brown Rice and Grilled Chicken Bowl	Seared Scallops with Citrus Dressing	Mixed Berry Parfait with Greek Yogurt
5	Veggie Omelet with Spinach and Tomatoes	Quinoa and Black Bean Salad	Lemon Herb Baked Tilapia	Banana Nice Cream with Almond Butter
6	Avocado Toast with Poached Egg	Baked Salmon with Dijon Mustard Glaze	Quinoa and Black Bean Stuffed Peppers	Baked Pears with Walnuts and Honey
7	Banana Walnut Muffins	Seared Tuna with Sesame Seeds	Seared Tuna with Sesame Seeds	Dark Chocolate-Dipped Strawberries

Week 5:

Day	Breakfast	Lunch	Dinner	Dessert
1	Oatmeal with Fresh Berries	Spaghetti Squash with Marinara Sauce	Veggie Stir-Fry with Tofu	Baked Apples with Cinnamon and Honey
2	Fruit Salad with Mint and Lime Dressing	Veggie Stir-Fry with Tofu	Baked Cod with Mango Salsa	Banana Oat Cookies
3	Veggie and Mushroom Scramble	Baked Cod with Mango Salsa	Baked Chicken Drumsticks with Herbs	Baked Pears with Walnuts and Honey
4	Greek Yogurt Parfait with Nuts and Honey	Baked Chicken Drumsticks with Herbs	Turkey Meatballs with Marinara Sauce	Dark Chocolate-Dipped Strawberries
5	Smoothie Bowl with Kale and Mixed Berries	Turkey Meatballs with Marinara Sauce	Baked Salmon with Dijon Mustard Glaze	Banana Nice Cream with Almond Butter
6	Vegetable Frittata with Egg Whites	Quinoa and Black Bean Stuffed Peppers	Quinoa and Black Bean Stuffed Peppers	Mango and Lime Sorbet
7	Chia Seed Pudding with Fruit Compote	Seared Tuna with Sesame Seeds	Seared Tuna with Sesame Seeds	Chia Seed Pudding with Coconut Milk & Fresh Fruit

Week 6:

Day	Breakfast	Lunch	Dinner	Dessert
1	Breakfast Burrito with Black Beans and Salsa	Spaghetti Squash with Marinara Sauce	Grilled Halibut with Mango Salsa	Mixed Berry Parfait with Greek Yogurt
2	Brown Rice Porridge with Cinnamon and Apples	Veggie Stir-Fry with Tofu	Veggie Stir-Fry with Tofu	Chia Seed Pudding with Coconut Milk & Fresh Fruit
3	Blueberry Almond Overnight Oats	Baked Cod with Mango Salsa	Quinoa and Black Bean Stuffed Peppers	Mango and Lime Sorbet
4	Whole Grain Pancakes with Fresh Fruit Toppings	Baked Chicken Drumsticks with Herbs	Turkey Meatballs with Marinara Sauce	Banana Nice Cream with Almond Butter
5	Veggie Omelet with Spinach and Tomatoes	Turkey Meatballs with Marinara Sauce	Baked Salmon with Dijon Mustard Glaze	Baked Pears with Walnuts and Honey
6	Avocado Toast with Poached Egg	Quinoa and Black Bean Stuffed Peppers	Quinoa and Black Bean Stuffed Peppers	Dark Chocolate-Dipped Strawberries
7	Banana Walnut Muffins	Seared Tuna with Sesame Seeds	Seared Tuna with Sesame Seeds	Baked Apples with Cinnamon and Honey

Week 7:

Day	Breakfast	Lunch	Dinner	Dessert
1	Oatmeal with Fresh Berries	Veggie Stir-Fry with Tofu	Veggie Stir-Fry with Tofu	Mango and Lime Sorbet
2	Fruit Salad with Mint and Lime Dressing	Baked Cod with Mango Salsa	Grilled Halibut with Mango Salsa	Chia Seed Pudding with Coconut Milk & Fresh Fruit
3	Veggie and Mushroom Scramble	Quinoa and Black Bean Stuffed Peppers	Turkey Meatballs with Marinara Sauce	Mixed Berry Parfait with Greek Yogurt
4	Greek Yogurt Parfait with Nuts and Honey	Turkey Meatballs with Marinara Sauce	Baked Salmon with Dijon Mustard Glaze	Banana Nice Cream with Almond Butter
5	Smoothie Bowl with Kale and Mixed Berries	Baked Chicken Drumsticks with Herbs	Quinoa and Black Bean Stuffed Peppers	Baked Pears with Walnuts and Honey
6	Vegetable Frittata with Egg Whites	Quinoa and Black Bean Stuffed Peppers	Baked Cod with Mango Salsa	Dark Chocolate-Dipped Strawberries
7	Chia Seed Pudding with Fruit Compote	Seared Tuna with Sesame Seeds	Seared Tuna with Sesame Seeds	Baked Apples with Cinnamon and Honey

Week 8:

Day	Breakfast	Lunch	Dinner	Dessert
1	Breakfast Burrito with Black Beans and Salsa	Turkey and Vegetable Stir-Fry	Grilled Skinless Chicken Breast with Herbs	Mango and Lime Sorbet
2	Brown Rice Porridge with Cinnamon and Apples	Chickpea and Roasted Vegetable Bowl	Baked Pork Tenderloin with Apple Chutney	Chia Seed Pudding with Coconut Milk & Fresh Fruit
3	Blueberry Almond Overnight Oats	Thai Shrimp Lettuce Wraps	Beef Stir-Fry with Broccoli and Snow Peas	Mixed Berry Parfait with Greek Yogurt
4	Whole Grain Pancakes with Fresh Fruit Toppings	Brown Rice and Grilled Chicken Bowl	Seared Scallops with Citrus Dressing	Banana Nice Cream with Almond Butter
5	Veggie Omelet with Spinach and Tomatoes	Quinoa and Black Bean Salad	Lemon Herb Baked Tilapia	Baked Pears with Walnuts and Honey
6	Avocado Toast with Poached Egg	Baked Salmon with Dijon Mustard Glaze	Quinoa and Black Bean Stuffed Peppers	Dark Chocolate-Dipped Strawberries
7	Banana Walnut Muffins	Seared Tuna with Sesame Seeds	Seared Tuna with Sesame Seeds	Chia Seed Pudding with Coconut Milk & Fresh Fruit

Conversion Chart

Volume Equivalents (Liquid)

US Standard	US Standard (oz)	Metric (approximate)
two tbsps	1 fl. oz	30 milliliter
quarter teacup	2 fl. oz	60 milliliter
half teacup	4 fl. oz	120 milliliter
one teacup	8 fl. oz	240 milliliter
one and half teacups	12 fl. oz	355 milliliter
two teacups or one pint	16 fl. oz	475 milliliter
four teacups or one quart	32 fl. oz	1 Liter
one gallon	128 fl. oz	4 Liter

Volume Equivalents (Dry)

US Standard	Metric (approximate)
one-eighth tsp	0.5 milliliter
quarter tsp	1 milliliter
half tsp	2 milliliter
three-quarter tsp	4 milliliter
one tsp	5 milliliter
one tbsp	15 milliliter
quarter teacup	59 milliliter
one-third teacup	79 milliliter
half teacup	118 milliliter
two-third teacup	156 milliliter
three-quarter teacup	177 milliliter
one teacup	235 milliliter
two teacups or one pint	475 milliliter
three teacups	700 milliliter
four teacups or one quart	1 Liter

Oven Temperatures

Fahrenheit (F)	Celsius (C) (approximate)
250 deg.F	120 deg.C
300 deg.F	150 deg.C
325 deg.F	165 deg.C
350 deg.F	180 deg.C
375 deg.F	190 deg.C
400 deg.F	200 deg.C
425 deg.F	220 deg.C
450 deg.F	230 deg.C

Weight Equivalents

US Standard	Metric (approximate)
one tbsp	15gm
half oz	15gm
one oz	30gm
two oz	60gm
four oz	115gm
eight oz	225gm
twelve oz	340gm
sixteen oz or one lb.	455gm

Recipes Index

Conclusion

Fatty liver is a common liver condition characterized by an abnormal accumulation of fat within the liver cells. While small amounts of fat in the liver are normal and essential for its functions, excessive fat buildup can lead to health complications. Fatty liver has two primary forms: alcoholic fatty liver disease (AFLD) & nonalcoholic fatty liver disease (NAFLD). AFLD is associated with chronic alcohol consumption, while NAFLD is linked to factors like obesity, insulin resistance, and metabolic disorders.

Fatty liver is often asymptomatic in its early stages, making it crucial for individuals at risk to undergo regular medical check-ups and screenings. The disease can progress to more severe conditions, such as NASH, cirrhosis, liver failure, and liver cancer if left untreated.

The management & prevention of fatty liver disease revolve around lifestyle modifications, particularly diet and weight management. A fatty liver diet emphasizes consuming nutrient-dense foods while avoiding those that contribute to fat accumulation in the liver. Weight control is essential, as excess body weight is a significant risk factor for NAFLD.

Dietary choices that improve insulin sensitivity, reduce fat accumulation, and support liver health can be beneficial in managing fatty liver. Including antioxidants, healthy fats, fatty fish, whole grains, and herbal teas can promote liver health. On the other hand, limiting saturated fats, refined carbohydrates, and added sugars is crucial to prevent fat buildup in the liver.

Incorporating a healthy diet and engaging in regular physical activity not only benefits the liver but also supports overall well-being. Proper nutrition can improve energy levels, strengthen the immune system, and reduce the risk of other chronic diseases.

Fatty liver disease should not be taken lightly, and those at risk should seek guidance from healthcare professionals or registered dietitians to create personalized nutrition plans. By making appropriate dietary choices and adopting a healthy lifestyle, individuals can effectively manage, prevent, and potentially reverse fatty liver disease, safeguarding liver health and overall well-being.

Printed in Great Britain
by Amazon

35836050R00057